Z 711.2 .I26 1999
Iannuzzi, Patricia
Teaching information
literary skills

Teaching
Information
Literacy Skills

DISCARD

CORETTE LIBRARY CARROLL COLLEGE

Teaching Information Literacy Skills

PATRICIA IANNUZZI
Florida International University

CHARLES T. MANGRUM II
University of Miami–Coral Gables

STEPHEN S. STRICHART
Florida International University

Allyn and Bacon
Boston   London   Toronto   Sydney   Tokyo   Singapore

Series editorial assistant: Mark Listenik
Marketing managers: Ellen Dolberg and Brad Parkins

Copyright © 1999 by Allyn & Bacon
A Viacom Company
Needham Heights, MA 02494

Internet: www.abacon.com

All rights reserved. No part of the material protected by this copyright notice may be reproduced or utilized in any form or by any means, electronic or mechanical, including photocopying, recording, or by any information storage and retrieval system, without written permission from the copyright owner.

The reproducible masters contained within may be reproduced for use with this book, provided such reproductions bear copyright notice, but may not be reproduced in any other form for any other purpose without permission from the copyright owner.

Some of the activities in this book have been adapted from the following: *Teaching Study Skills and Strategies in High School* by Stephen S. Strichart, Charles T. Mangrum II, and Patricia Iannuzzi, copyright © 1997 by Allyn and Bacon; *Teaching Study Skills and Strategies in Grades 4–8* by Charles T. Mangrum II, Patricia Iannuzzi, and Stephen S. Strichart, copyright © 1997 by Allyn and Bacon; and *Teaching Study Skills and Strategies in College* by Patricia Iannuzzi, Stephen S. Strichart, and Charles T. Mangrum II, copyright © 1998 by Allyn and Bacon.

In regard to the software disk accompanying this text, the publisher assumes no responsibility for damages, errors, or omissions, without any limitation, which may result from the use of the program or the text.

Library of Congress Cataloging-in-Publication Data

Iannuzzi, Patricia.
    Teaching information literacy skills / Patricia Iannuzzi, Charles T. Mangrum II, Stephen S. Strichart.
       p.   cm.
    Includes bibliographical references (p.).
    ISBN 0-205-28007-2
    1. Library orientation for high school students—United States.
    2. Library orientation for college students—United States.
    3. Library orientation for junior high school students—United States.   4. Information retrieval—Study and teaching (Secondary)—United States.   5. Information retrieval—Study and teaching (Higher)—United States.   6. Report writing—Study and teaching (Secondary)—United States.   7. Report writing—Study and teaching (Higher)—United States.   I. Mangrum, Charles T.   II. Strichart, Stephen S.   III. Title.
Z711.2.I26   1999
025.5'6—dc21
                                                         98-35027
                                                           CIP

Printed in the United States of America

10 9 8 7 6 5 4 3 2 1   02 01 00 99 98

Contents

Introduction xi

Information Literacy xi
How This Book Will Help xi
Information Literacy Skills Taught in This Book xii
About the Reproducible Activities xiii
How This Book Is Organized xviii
How to Use This Book xix
Teaching Notes xix

Acknowledgments xxi

About the Authors xxiii

CHAPTER ONE
Accessing Information 1

Chapter Objectives 1
Titles of Reproducible Activities 1
Using the Reproducible Activities 2

1-1   A Strategy for Using Information Literacy Skills   9
1-2   Information Literacy and Research   11
1-3   Learning about Tools to Find Information   12
1-4   Using a Card Catalog   14
1-5   Using an Online Catalog   15
1-6   Using Your Online Catalog   16
1-7   Learning about Print Indexes and Electronic Databases   17
1-8   Learning about Types of Print Indexes and Electronic Databases   18
1-9   Using Print Indexes and Electronic Databases   19
1-10 Learning about Keywords   21
1-11 Learning about Boolean Connectors   22
1-12 Using Keywords and Boolean Connectors to Research Your Topic   23
1-13 Learning about Truncation   24
1-14 Searching by Proximity   25
1-15 Learning about Controlled Vocabulary   27
1-16 Using Controlled Vocabulary   28

1-17	Limiting by Date and Language	29
1-18	Using Date and Language Limits	31
1-19	Marking, Printing, Downloading, and Sending	32
1-20	Using Advanced Search Strategy Techniques	33
	Answer Key 34	

CHAPTER TWO
Locating and Using Materials 36
Chapter Objectives 36
Titles of Reproducible Activities 36
Using the Reproducible Activities 36

2-1	Formats of Information	40
2-2	Types of Materials Found in a Library	41
2-3	Using Microforms	42
2-4	Learning about Call Numbers	43
2-5	Learning about the Dewey Decimal System	44
2-6	Learning about the Library of Congress System	45
2-7	Learning about Popular Magazines and Scholarly Journals	46
2-8	Using Popular Magazines and Scholarly Journals	47
2-9	Learning about Government Documents	48
2-10	Using Government Documents	49
2-11	Learning about Primary Sources	50
2-12	Using Primary Sources	51
	Answer Key 52	

CHAPTER THREE
Using Reference Sources 53
Chapter Objectives 53
Titles of Reproducible Activities 53
Using the Reproducible Activities 54

3-1	Learning about Reference Sources	61
3-2	Learning about Electronic Reference Sources	63
3-3	Locating Print and Electronic Dictionaries	64
3-4	Using a Dictionary	66
3-5	Comparing Information from Dictionaries	68
3-6	Locating Print and Electronic Encyclopedias	69
3-7	Using a Print Encyclopedia	71
3-8	Comparing Information from Print Encyclopedias	72
3-9	Using a Multimedia Encyclopedia	73
3-10	Comparing Information from Print and Multimedia Encyclopedias	75
3-11	Locating Almanacs	76
3-12	Using Almanacs	77
3-13	Locating Statistical Sources	78
3-14	Using Statistical Abstract of the United States	79
3-15	Locating Print and Electronic Atlases	80
3-16	Using Print Atlases	81
3-17	Using Electronic Atlases	82
3-18	Locating Biographical Sources	83
3-19	Using Biographical Sources	84

3-20	Locating Chronologies	85
3-21	Using Chronologies	86
3-22	Locating Reference Sources for Literary Criticism	87
3-23	Using Reference Sources for Literary Criticism	88
3-24	Using Reference Sources	89
	Answer Key	90

CHAPTER FOUR
Interpreting Visual Information from Reference Sources   92

Chapter Objectives   92
Titles of Reproducible Activities   92
Using the Reproducible Activities   92

4-1	Tables	96
4-2	Another Table	97
4-3	A Complex Table	98
4-4	Bar Graphs	99
4-5	Line Graphs	100
4-6	Pie Graphs	101
4-7	Organizational Charts	102
4-8	Time Lines	103
4-9	Diagrams	104
4-10	Political and Physical Maps	105
4-11	Data Maps	106
	Answer Key	107

CHAPTER FIVE
Using the Internet   108

Chapter Objectives   108
Titles of Reproducible Activities   108
Using the Reproducible Activities   109

5-1	A Strategy for Using Information Literacy Skills	115
5-2	Learning about the Internet	116
5-3	Learning about E-mail	118
5-4	Advanced E-mail	119
5-5	Using E-mail	120
5-6	Practicing Netiquette	121
5-7	Learning about the World Wide Web	123
5-8	Using URLs on the WWW	125
5-9	Tourist Attractions to Explore on the WWW	126
5-10	Schools to Explore on the WWW	127
5-11	Libraries to Explore on the WWW	128
5-12	Reference Sources on the WWW	129
5-13	Government Sources on the WWW	130
5-14	Primary Sources on the WWW	131
5-15	Learning about Your Local FreeNet	132
5-16	Using Your Local FreeNet	134
5-17	Learning about Search Engines and Directories	135
5-18	Using a Search Engine or Directory	137
	Answer Key	138

CHAPTER SIX
Evaluating Information 140
Chapter Objectives 140
Titles of Reproducible Activities 140
Using the Reproducible Activities 140
- 6-1 A Checklist for Evaluating Information from Library Sources 143
- 6-2 Evaluating Information from Library Sources on a Topic 145
- 6-3 Evaluating Information from Library Sources on Your Topic 146
- 6-4 A Checklist for Evaluating Information from the WWW 147
- 6-5 Evaluating Information from the WWW on a Topic 149
- 6-6 Evaluating Information from the WWW on Your Topic 150
- 6-7 Evaluating WWW Sites 151
- 6-8 Evaluating More WWW Sites 152
- Answer Key 153

CHAPTER SEVEN
Writing a Research Paper 154
Chapter Objectives 154
Titles of Reproducible Activities 154
Using the Reproducible Activities 154
- 7-1 A Strategy for Writing a Research Paper 158
- 7-2 Choosing a Topic 159
- 7-3 Informative and Persuasive Topics 160
- 7-4 Practice Writing Persuasive Topics 161
- 7-5 Focusing Your Research 162
- 7-6 Locating Sources of Information 163
- 7-7 Preparing Bibliography Cards 164
- 7-8 Preparing Note Cards 165
- 7-9 Writing the Outline 166
- 7-10 Writing the Draft 167
- 7-11 Revising the Draft 168
- 7-12 Preparing Footnotes 169
- 7-13 Preparing the Title Page 170
- 7-14 Preparing the Table of Contents 171
- 7-15 Preparing the Bibliography 172
- 7-16 Final Checklist 173
- Answer Key 174

CHAPTER EIGHT
Using Resources for Oral Presentations 175
Chapter Objectives 175
Titles of Reproducible Activities 175
Using the Reproducible Activities 175
- 8-1 Locating Print Sources for Quotations 178
- 8-2 Using Print Sources for Quotations 179
- 8-3 Quotations on the WWW 180
- 8-4 Locating Speeches in Print 181
- 8-5 Locating Speeches in Audio/Visual Formats 182
- 8-6 Locating Sources for Opposing Viewpoints 183

8-7	Helpful WWW Sources for Oral Presentations	184
	Answer Key 185	

Bibliography   187

APPENDIX A
Information Literacy Curriculum   193

Order Form   199

Introduction

INFORMATION LITERACY

According to the American Library Association (ALA), an information-literate person is able to "recognize when information is needed and have the ability to locate, evaluate, and use effectively the needed information."[1] The American Association of School Librarians (AASL), a division of ALA, adopted a curriculum for information literacy skills that was developed by the Wisconsin Educational Media Association. This curriculum was also adopted by the National Forum on Information Literacy (NFIL), an umbrella group of over sixty education organizations representing K–12 and higher education. This curriculum, and variations of it, is being used by colleges and school systems throughout the United States. Increasingly, accreditation criteria also include information literacy competencies. Teachers, college instructors, librarians, and school media specialists must work together to integrate information literacy skills into all curriculum areas.

HOW THIS BOOK WILL HELP

This book provides reproducible activities to help students master information literacy skills important for success in all subjects. The reproducible activities provide opportunities for active learning in the classroom, library, and computer laboratory. Teaching students information literacy skills is an important step in developing lifelong learners in an increasingly complex, technology-based learning environment.

Accompanying this book is a trial version of a computer assessment titled Information Literacy Assessment (ILA). ILA is a self-assessment of students' use of the information literacy skills taught in this book. The free trial disk,

---

[1] American Library Association Presidential Committee on Information Literacy, Final Report. (Chicago: American Library Association, 1989)

available in Windows only, allows you to administer ILA to five students. After five administrations, the trial disk is no longer usable. You may purchase a disk with unlimited administrations in either Windows or Macintosh formats. The order form is at the end of this book.

INFORMATION LITERACY SKILLS TAUGHT IN THIS BOOK

Activities for teaching the information literacy skills are presented in eight chapters:

Chapter One
Accessing Information

In this chapter, students are taught a strategy for accessing information. They are taught how to use print and electronic tools to access information as well as techniques to do effective computer searches.

Chapter Two
Locating and Using Materials

In this chapter, students are taught about formats of information and the different types of materials found in libraries. They are also taught how to locate materials within a library.

Chapter Three
Using Reference Sources

In this chapter, students are taught about the different categories of reference sources. They are also taught to use the print and electronic formats of these sources.

Chapter Four
Interpreting Visual Information from Reference Sources

In this chapter, students are introduced to different ways that information can be presented visually. They are also taught how to interpret information presented in various visual formats.

Chapter Five
Using the Internet

In this chapter, students are taught about the different kinds of information that can be found on the World Wide Web (WWW). They are taught to use effective search strategies when searching for information on the WWW. They are also taught how to use e-mail to communicate on the Internet.

Chapter Six
Evaluating Information

In this chapter, students are taught to use criteria for evaluating information found in the library and on the WWW.

Chapter Seven
Writing a Research Paper

In this chapter students are taught a series of steps to follow as they write a research paper.

Chapter Eight
Using Resources for Oral Presentations

In this chapter students are taught about specialized print and electronic reference sources they can use when preparing oral presentations. They are also taught about resources on the WWW they can use as they prepare oral presentations.

ABOUT THE REPRODUCIBLE ACTIVITIES

The activities in this book are consistent with the information literacy curriculum currently adopted by the AASL (see Appendix A). Table I-1 is a matrix showing the correspondence between activities in this book and the components of that information literacy curriculum.

The columns in the matrix represent seven areas of the information literacy curriculum:[2]

   I. Defining the need for information
   II. Initiating the search strategy
   III. Locating the resources
   IV. Assessing and comprehending the information
   V. Interpreting the information
   VI. Communicating the information
   VII. Evaluating the product and process

---

[2] American Library Association. American Association of School Libraries. Position Paper on Information Literacy. http://www.ala.org/aasl/positions/PS_infolit.html 5 January 1998. Appendix A contains the full text of the information literacy curriculum developed by the Wisconsin Educational Media Association and adopted by the American Association of School Librarians, a division of ALA.

Table I-1 Correspondence Between Reproducible Activities and Components of the Information Literacy Curriculum

Reproducible Activity Number and Title	Defining the Need for Information	Initiating the Search Strategy	Locating the Resources	Assessing and Comprehending the Information	Interpreting the Information	Communicating the Information	Evaluate the Product and the Process
1-1 A Strategy for Using Information Literacy Skills	✔						*
1-2 Information Literacy and Research	✔						*
1-3 Learning about Tools to Find Information		✔	✔				*
1-4 Using a Card Catalog			✔				*
1-5 Using an Online Catalog			✔				*
1-6 Using Your Online Catalog			✔				*
1-7 Learning about Print Indexes and Electronic Databases			✔				*
1-8 Learning about Types of Print Indexes and Electronic Databases			✔				*
1-9 Using Print Indexes and Electronic Databases			✔				*
1-10 Learning about Keywords		✔					*
1-11 Learning about Boolean Connectors		✔					*
1-12 Using Keywords and Boolean Connectors to Research Your Topic		✔					*
1-13 Learning about Truncation		✔					*
1-14 Searching by Proximity		✔	✔				*
1-15 Learning about Controlled Vocabulary		✔					*
1-16 Using Controlled Vocabulary		✔	✔				✔
1-17 Limiting by Date and Language		✔					*
1-18 Using Date and Language Limits		✔	✔				✔
1-19 Marking, Printing, Downloading, and Sending		✔	✔				*
1-20 Using Advanced Search Strategy Techniques		✔	✔				*
2-1 Formats of Information			✔				*
2-2 Types of Materials Found in a Library			✔				*
2-3 Using Microforms			✔				✔
2-4 Learning about Call Numbers			✔				*
2-5 Learning about the Dewey Decimal System			✔				*
2-6 Learning about the Library of Congress System			✔				*
2-7 Learning about Popular Magazines and Scholarly Journals			✔				*
2-8 Using Popular Magazines and Scholarly Journals	✔	✔	✔	✔	✔		*
2-9 Learning about Government Documents			✔				*
2-10 Using Government Documents			✔				*
2-11 Learning about Primary Sources				✔			*
2-12 Using Primary Sources		✔	✔	✔	✔		*
3-1 Learning about Reference Sources		✔	✔				*
3-2 Learning about Electronic Reference Sources		✔					*

*Each reproducible activity meets this component when the instructor provides feedback and opportunities for student reflection.

Table I-1 Correspondence Between Reproducible Activities and Components of the Information Literacy Curriculum (*continued*)

Reproducible Activity Number and Title	Defining the Need for Information	Initiating the Search Strategy	Locating the Resources	Assessing and Comprehending the Information	Interpreting the Information	Communicating the Information	Evaluate the Product and the Process
3-3 Locating Print and Electronic Dictionaries		✓	✓				*
3-4 Using a Dictionary			✓				*
3-5 Comparing Information from Dictionaries			✓	✓	✓		*
3-6 Locating Print and Electronic Encyclopedias		✓	✓				*
3-7 Using a Print Encyclopedia		✓					*
3-8 Comparing Information from Print Encyclopedias		✓	✓	✓	✓		✓
3-9 Using a Multimedia Encyclopedia		✓	✓	✓			*
3-10 Comparing Information from Print and Multimedia Encyclopedias		✓	✓	✓	✓	✓	✓
3-11 Locating Almanacs			✓				*
3-12 Using Almanacs		✓	✓	✓			✓
3-13 Locating Statistical Sources		✓	✓				*
3-14 Using Statistical Abstract of the United States		✓	✓	✓			*
3-15 Locating Print and Electronic Atlases		✓	✓				*
3-16 Using Print Atlases			✓	✓			*
3-17 Using Electronic Atlases		✓	✓	✓			*
3-18 Locating Biographical Sources		✓	✓				*
3-19 Using Biographical Sources		✓	✓	✓			*
3-20 Locating Chronologies		✓	✓				*
3-21 Using Chronologies		✓	✓	✓			*
3-22 Locating Reference Sources for Literary Criticism		✓	✓				*
3-23 Using Reference Sources for Literary Criticism		✓	✓	✓	✓	✓	*
3-24 Using Reference Sources		✓					*
4-1 Tables			✓	✓			*
4-2 Another Table			✓	✓			*
4-3 A Complex Table			✓	✓			*
4-4 Bar Graphs			✓	✓			*
4-5 Line Graphs			✓	✓			*
4-6 Pie Graphs			✓	✓			*
4-7 Organizational Charts			✓	✓			*
4-8 Time Lines			✓	✓			*
4-9 Diagrams			✓	✓			*
4-10 Political and Physical Maps			✓	✓			*
4-11 Data Maps			✓	✓			*
5-1 A Strategy for Using Information Literacy Skills	✓						*

*Each reproducible activity meets this component when the instructor provides feedback and opportunities for student reflection.

(*continued*)

Table I-1 Correspondence Between Reproducible Activities and Components of the Information Literacy Curriculum (*continued*)

Reproducible Activity Number and Title	Defining the Need for Information	Initiating the Search Strategy	Locating the Resources	Assessing and Comprehending the Information	Interpreting the Information	Communicating the Information	Evaluate the Product and the Process
5-2 Learning about the Internet			✔				*
5-3 Learning about E-mail			✔				*
5-4 Advanced E-mail			✔				*
5-5 Using E-mail			✔				*
5-6 Practicing Netiquette							*
5-7 Learning about the World Wide Web			✔				*
5-8 Using URLs on the WWW			✔				*
5-9 Tourist Attractions to Explore on the WWW			✔	✔	✔		*
5-10 Schools to Explore on the WWW			✔	✔	✔		*
5-11 Libraries to Explore on the WWW			✔	✔	✔		*
5-12 Reference Sources on the WWW			✔	✔	✔		*
5-13 Government Sources on the WWW			✔	✔	✔		*
5-14 Primary Sources on the WWW			✔	✔	✔		*
5-15 Learning about Your Local FreeNet			✔	✔			*
5-16 Using Your Local FreeNet			✔		✔		*
5-17 Learning about Search Engines and Directories			✔	✔	✔		*
5-18 Using a Search Engine or Directory		✔	✔				*
6-1 A Checklist for Evaluating Information from Library Sources	✔	✔		✔	✔	✔	*
6-2 Evaluating Information from Library Sources on a Topic	✔	✔		✔	✔	✔	*
6-3 Evaluating Information from Library Sources on Your Topic	✔	✔	✔	✔	✔	✔	*
6-4 A Checklist for Evaluating Information from the WWW	✔	✔		✔	✔	✔	*
6-5 Evaluating Information from the WWW on a Topic	✔	✔		✔	✔	✔	*
6-6 Evaluating Information from the WWW on Your Topic	✔	✔	✔	✔	✔	✔	*
6-7 Evaluating WWW Sites	✔	✔	✔	✔	✔	✔	*
6-8 Evaluating More WWW Sites	✔	✔	✔	✔	✔	✔	*
7-1 A Strategy for Writing a Research Paper	✔						*
7-2 Choosing a Topic	✔	✔					*
7-3 Informative and Persuasive Topics	✔	✔					*
7-4 Practice Writing Persuasive Topics	✔	✔					*
7-5 Focusing Your Research	✔	✔					*
7-6 Locating Sources of Information	✔	✔	✔				*
7-7 Preparing Bibliography Cards						✔	*
7-8 Preparing Note Cards				✔	✔	✔	*
7-9 Writing the Outline					✔	✔	*

*Each reproducible activity meets this component when the instructor provides feedback and opportunities for student reflection.

Table I-1 Correspondence Between Reproducible Activities and Components of the Information Literacy Curriculum (*continued*)

Reproducible Activity Number and Title	Defining the Need for Information	Initiating the Search Strategy	Locating the Resources	Assessing and Comprehending the Information	Interpreting the Information	Communicating the Information	Evaluate the Product and the Process
7-10 Writing the Draft				✔	✔	✔	*
7-11 Revising the Draft				✔	✔	✔	✔
7-12 Preparing Footnotes						✔	*
7-13 Preparing the Title Page						✔	*
7-14 Preparing the Table of Contents				✔	✔	✔	*
7-15 Preparing the Bibliography						✔	*
7-16 Final Checklist							✔
8-1 Locating Print Sources for Quotations			✔				*
8-2 Using Print Sources for Quotations			✔				
8-3 Quotations on the WWW			✔	✔	✔	✔	✔
8-4 Locating Speeches in Print			✔				*
8-5 Locating Speeches in Audio/Visual Formats	✔		✔	✔	✔	✔	*
8-6 Locating Sources for Opposing Viewpoints			✔				*
8-7 Helpful WWW Sources for Oral Presentations			✔	✔	✔	✔	*

*Each reproducible activity meets this component when the instructor provides feedback and opportunities for student reflection.

Information literacy curricula are under continual review by the organizations that adopt them. AASL and the Association for Educational Communications and Technology (AECT) have issued a draft document, *Information Literacy Standards for Student Learning*. The information literacy category contains three standards related to accessing, evaluating, and using information.[3] The activities in this book are also consistent with the skills identified in this draft document.

---

[3]American Library Association. AASL/AECT National Guidelines Vision Committee. Information Literacy Standards for Student Learning. Draft #5. http://www.ala.org/aasl/stndsdrft5.html 5 January 1998.

HOW THIS BOOK IS ORGANIZED

The first activity in Chapter One presents a flowchart describing a strategy for using information literacy skills. Chapters in this book address various parts of the flowchart. This flowchart is reproduced here with shaded areas corresponding to specific chapters. The chapter numbers are indicated in white boxes within each shaded area.

Chapters are organized as follows:

1. Objectives
2. Titles of Reproducible Activities
3. Using the Reproducible Activities
4. Reproducible Activities
5. Answers for Reproducible Activities

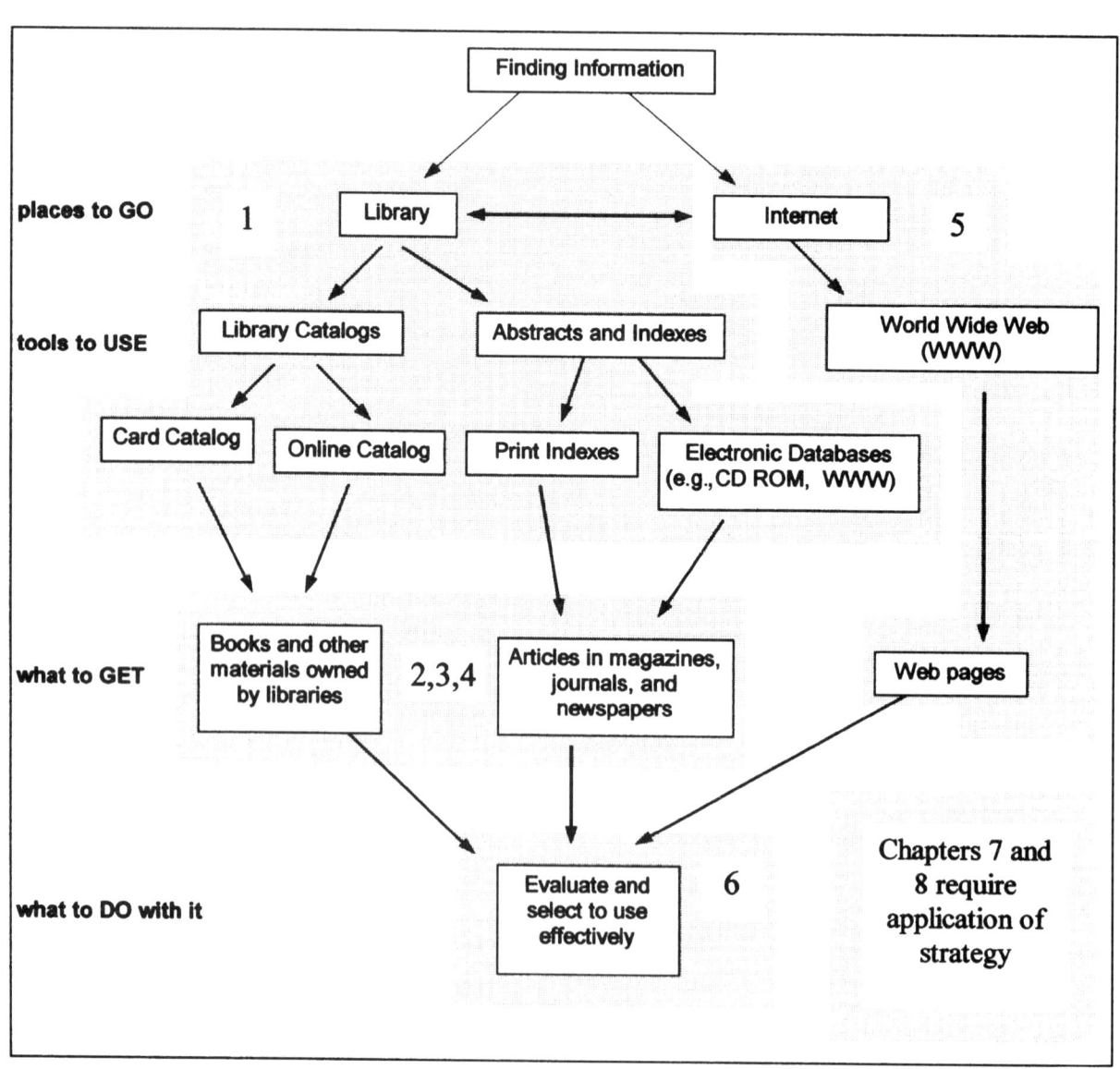

HOW TO USE THIS BOOK

1. Use the results from ILA to select the chapters and activities most appropriate for your students.
2. Duplicate the reproducible activities you wish to use.
3. Use the suggestions found in Using the Reproducible Activities and your own ideas to provide instruction.
4. Whenever possible, use content from real assignments in different subjects.

TEACHING NOTES

1. Go beyond the reproducibles to provide your students with additional practice within the context of a class assignment. Relating the activities to classroom objectives will enable students to achieve greater success.
2. Some of the activities require the students to have an information need already identified. Use real assignments from classes where an information need is already defined.
3. Some of the activities provide a topic for students to use to complete the activity. You may use the topic provided, substitute a topic from a specific class, or extend the activity by doing both.
4. Activities labeled with $\boxed{L}$ require the students to go to the library.

   Activities labeled with $\boxed{C}$ require the students to use a computer.

   Activities without a label can be done in a classroom without using a computer.

Acknowledgments

We express our appreciation to our colleagues at Florida International University and the University of Miami who graciously gave their time to review the activities in this book. Their reactions and recommendations were of great assistance to us. We also wish to acknowledge our students, whose feedback about the activities allowed us to make important improvements.

About the Authors

Patricia Iannuzzi is head of the Reference Department and co-director of the Information Literacy Initiative at Florida International University Libraries. She graduated from Yale University and earned an M.S. in Library and Information Science at Simmons College in 1980. Ms. Iannuzzi has worked in libraries at Tufts University, Yale University, and the University of California at Berkeley, where she was a Council on Library Resources (CLR) management intern. Since 1990, she has been on the library faculty at Florida International University, where she manages reference services, teaches a Freshman Experience seminar, and teaches information literacy skills in subjects across the curriculum.

Charles T. Mangrum II is professor of special education and reading at the University of Miami, Coral Gables, Florida. He graduated from Northern Michigan University and taught elementary and secondary school before entering graduate school. He earned an Ed.D. from Indiana University in 1968. Since 1968, he has been on the faculty at the University of Miami, where he trains teachers who teach students with reading and learning disabilities. Dr. Mangrum is the author of many books, instructional programs, and articles on topics related to reading and study skills.

Stephen S. Strichart is professor of special education and learning disabilities at Florida International University, Miami. He graduated from City College of New York and taught children with various types of disabilities before entering graduate school. Dr. Strichart earned a Ph.D. from Yeshiva University in 1972. Since 1975, he has been on the faculty at Florida International University, where he trains teachers and psychologists to work with exceptional students. Dr. Strichart is the author of many books and articles on topics related to special education and study skills.

CHAPTER ONE

Accessing Information

CHAPTER OBJECTIVES

1. Teach students to use print and electronic tools in the library to access information.
2. Teach students techniques in order to do effective computer searches.

TITLES OF REPRODUCIBLE ACTIVITIES

- **1-1** A Strategy for Using Information Literacy Skills
- **1-2** Information Literacy and Research
- **1-3** Learning about Tools to Find Information
- **1-4** Using a Card Catalog
- **1-5** Using an Online Catalog
- **1-6** Using Your Online Catalog
- **1-7** Learning about Print Indexes and Electronic Databases
- **1-8** Learning about Types of Print Indexes and Electronic Databases
- **1-9** Using Print Indexes and Electronic Databases
- **1-10** Learning about Keywords
- **1-11** Learning about Boolean Connectors
- **1-12** Using Keywords and Boolean Connectors to Research Your Topic
- **1-13** Learning about Truncation
- **1-14** Searching by Proximity
- **1-15** Learning about Controlled Vocabulary
- **1-16** Using Controlled Vocabulary
- **1-17** Limiting by Date and Language
- **1-18** Using Date and Language Limits
- **1-19** Marking, Printing, Downloading, and Sending
- **1-20** Using Advanced Search Strategy Techniques
  Answer Key

USING THE REPRODUCIBLE ACTIVITIES

Use activities 1-1 and 1-2 to introduce students to the library and the Internet as places to find information, to define information literacy and research, and to have students think about the skills they already possess and determine how they will need those skills for their classwork. Activities 1-3 through 1-9 teach students to use the various print and electronic tools to access information in the library. Use activities 1-10 through 1-20 to teach students how to structure a search statement regardless of the search engine they are using and to apply what they have learned to specific search engines in their library.

1-1 A Strategy for Using Information Literacy Skills

Discuss with students how today's library contains information in both print and electronic form. Guide students through the flowchart and define any terms they do not know. Explain the difference between tools to identify information and the information itself. Emphasize the difference between information found on web pages and in books, magazines, and other materials found in a library. Then have students read about the library and the Internet and write a paragraph that summarizes their experiences using the library and the Internet to find information. Ask students to share what they wrote.

1-2 Information Literacy and Research

Explain the relationship between research and information literacy. Then have students read the introductory text and complete the activity. By reviewing their projects and identifying those that require library research, this activity will reinforce planning and time management for students.

1-3 Learning about Tools to Find Information

Explain to students about the three major types of tools they will use to identify information. You may refer students to the flowchart in activity 1-1. Have students read about print and electronic versions of these tools and answer any questions they might have. Then have students go to the library on their own to find and read any instructional or informational materials that will help them answer the questions about these tools in their library. Also tell them to ask the librarian if there are other instructional materials to help them learn about these tools in their library.

1-4 Using a Card Catalog

Use this activity even if your school does not have a card catalog. Your students may use other local libraries that still have card catalogs. If they do, they need to know about the three types of cards found in the card catalog.

Explain why three cards are necessary. Point out that all the subject headings for the item can be found at the bottom of each type of card (as shown on the author card). Tell students that the number in the upper left corner is the call number. Then have students answer the questions.

(Activities 2-4 through 2-6 teach students about call numbers.)

1-5 Using an Online Catalog

Use this activity even if your school does not have an online catalog. Your students may use other local libraries that have online catalogs. If they do, they need to know about records in an online catalog.

Tell students that all online catalogs contain records of items owned by the library. The information about each item is arranged on the record in fields. Explain that different online catalogs may present the information in different ways, but the fields of information included are always the same. For example, some catalogs use the word *subjects* and others use the word *descriptors*. Some online catalogs do not label the field name. The record may look just like a record in the card catalog.

Use this activity to explain to students the type of information found on a record. Then have students answer the questions about the sample record. You may bring copies of a record from your online catalog and from the local public library, or another local online catalog, for students to compare.

1-6 Using Your Online Catalog

Explain to students that online catalogs may contain more information than the records for the items owned. Some include information about materials "on order" or "in use" and some have specific "holdings" information about serials. Many online catalogs include other databases for citations or full text of articles and still others provide links to resources on the Internet. Provide any instructional material about the catalog at your school. Help students to answer the questions about their catalogs.

CHAPTER ONE

1-7 Learning about Print Indexes and Electronic Databases

Explain that print indexes are used to identify citations to articles in periodicals and newspapers by topic and that electronic databases are computerized versions of print indexes. Have students read about print indexes and electronic databases and answer the questions.

You can extend instruction by telling students about the types of print indexes and electronic databases available in their library. You can also tell them that there are many different electronic database products available for libraries to purchase. Some include citations and abstracts only, others include the full text of the article. Some cover all topics, some include only newspapers, and still others identify magazines in a specific subject. These products may be on CD ROM, online as part of a larger computer to which you connect, or on the Internet. Most of the Internet-based databases are on the World Wide Web (WWW). Explain how libraries pay for subscriptions to these databases, and that even if they are on the WWW for students to use, they are not "free."

1-8 Learning about Types of Print Indexes and Electronic Databases [L] [C]

Use the activity to have students locate specific electronic databases and the print indexes available in your library. Have students read about the categories of print indexes and electronic databases.

Explain that although many libraries now own electronic databases, most also have print indexes, and some may only have print indexes. Print indexes are still necessary to use to find articles in older publications. Most electronic databases only go back to the 1980s, and many libraries buy only the current years. Print indexes, however, go back as far as the nineteenth century. Also, print indexes are available for specific disciplines. For example, if the library has the Art Index only in print, and a student needs information from art magazines, this may be a better index to use than an electronic one that may include only a few art magazines.

If your library has a list of all the databases available, students can consult the list to answer the questions. Tell them the names of the print equivalents and send them to the actual index to look at it and answer the question about the dates owned.

1-9 Using Print Indexes and Electronic Databases

Use this activity to teach students how to interpret the information in a citation from a print index and from an electronic database record. Explain that print indexes, like electronic databases, include citations to articles from a specific list of periodical and newspaper titles covered by the index.

ACCESSING INFORMATION **5**

Have students read the introductory text. Use the labeled example to review the parts of a citation with students. Review the four steps to follow when using a print index. Explain that the library may not own all the magazines for the citations they find, and offer suggestions for what they can do when that happens (e.g., select another citation, look in another library). Then direct students to label the parts of the citation provided.

Use the second part of this activity to introduce students to the fields in a record from an electronic database. Have students read the introductory text. Use the labeled record to explain how the parts of the citation are placed into fields. Then have students answer the questions about the sample record.

Because records vary from database to database, you may want to extend this activity by showing students sample records from a variety of databases.

1-10 Learning about Keywords
1-11 Learning about Boolean Connectors
1-12 Using Keywords and Boolean Connectors to Research Your Topic

Use these three activities to explain that every kind of database used to find information requires knowledge of keywords and Boolean connectors. On-line catalogs, electronic databases for articles, multimedia reference sources such as encyclopedias, even searches on the World Wide Web require students to select keywords and put them together in a computer search using Boolean connectors.

Activity 1-10 introduces students to keywords. Because computers are very literal, an efficient computer search requires students to use all possible keywords, forms of the keyword (e.g., singular and plural, present and past tense) and synonyms or related words.

Explain keywords to students and have them read through the example provided. Then have students select three keywords from the topic provided. Have students complete the activity by placing the keywords in the box and writing other forms for each keyword as well as synonyms or related words. Help students brainstorm for words to place in the box, emphasizing the need for creativity.

Activity 1-11 shows how Boolean connectors are used to do a computer search with keywords. Use the Venn diagrams to explain the three Boolean connectors **and, or, not**. Explain to students the use of the parenthesis to "nest" their terms. Many interfaces require knowledge of nesting to do efficient searches. Explain the use of the parenthesis in the example. Direct students to complete the activity.

Activity 1-12 requires the students to develop a search statement using keyword, Boolean connectors, and nesting for a topic of their choice. Use this activity when the students have an assignment that requires them to find information.

1-13 Learning about Truncation

Explain that online catalogs, electronic databases, and search engines on the WWW all use truncation symbols. Use the introductory material and the example *teach** to explain truncation. Have students write forms of the truncated word *teach** (*teacher, teaching, teaches*). Similarly, use the truncation *librar**. Point out that databases use different truncation symbols. Then have students complete the activity.

Explain why *comput!* may not be the best way to truncate a word if the student wants to retrieve only *computer* or *computers*.

You may extend this activity by telling students about truncation symbols used by electronic tools in their library. You can also extend this activity by having students refer to the search strategy they wrote in 1-12 and rewrite it using truncation.

1-14 Searching by Proximity [C]

Use this activity to teach students three ways of searching by proximity: by adjacency, within a paragraph, and within specific fields. Point out that although *same, near,* and *with* are commonly used for proximity searching, databases may use them differently. Some may use *with* to mean the same field, others may mean the same sentence. Also demonstrate how (5w) means within five words and that any number can be used. Then have students use an electronic tool available in their library to complete the activity.

1-15 Learning about Controlled Vocabulary

Use this activity to explain to students about controlled vocabulary. Have students read the text and explain anything they do not understand. Use the sample record to point out the difference between keyword searching and searching by subject headings or descriptors. Help students answer the questions about the sample record.

You may extend this activity by bringing in sample records from an electronic tool in their library.

1-16 Using Controlled Vocabulary [C]

Direct students to apply what they have learned about controlled vocabulary to search the online catalog in their library. Have students read the introductory text about "false hits" and explain any concepts they do not understand. Review the four steps to help students understand how to identify controlled vocabulary terms. Then have students use their online catalog to complete the activity.

1-17 Limiting by Date and Language

Explain to students that most databases allow you to limit the search results by date and by language. Explain that the commands used by each database to limit will vary, but that the function is the same. Have students read about limiting, review the examples, and answer the question following each example.

You may extend this activity by providing additional examples of date and language limits from electronic tools in their library.

1-18 Using Date and Language Limits

Have students apply what they have learned about limiting by using the online catalog or an electronic database in their library. Direct students to answer the questions about the system they selected.

1-19 Marking, Printing, Downloading, and Sending

Explain to students that when they do a search, they may retrieve more records than they can use on their topic. Therefore, students may need to select the records they wish to use. Explain that they must mark the records that they select. Define the term *marking* and describe other terms that may be used by electronic tools for the same function (e.g., *select, tag*). Then describe the options available to students for "getting" the records they mark: printing, downloading, and sending to an e-mail address. Explain to students that every electronic database does this differently and that there are also many differences between libraries. It is important for students to understand that there may be differences so that they are not confused when they use other local libraries.

Then have students apply what they have learned by answering the questions about the online catalog or an electronic database in their library.

1-20 Using Advanced Search Strategy Techniques

The checklist in 1-20 requires students to apply many of the skills they have learned in this chapter. Encourage teachers to have students complete this checklist when turning in an assignment that requires use of the online catalog or an electronic database. Students should not turn in an assignment until they have checked every item on the checklist.

You may extend this activity by requiring students to attach copies of their search strategies or results.

A Strategy for Using Information Literacy Skills   1-1

Information literacy is the ability to identify, locate, evaluate, and select information in all formats in order to use it effectively. Information literacy expands upon basic literacy and computer literacy. To be information literate, you must know how to use the tools and services available in the library and on the Internet. You must also know how to evaluate the information that you find.

The following flowchart shows a strategy for using information literacy skills.

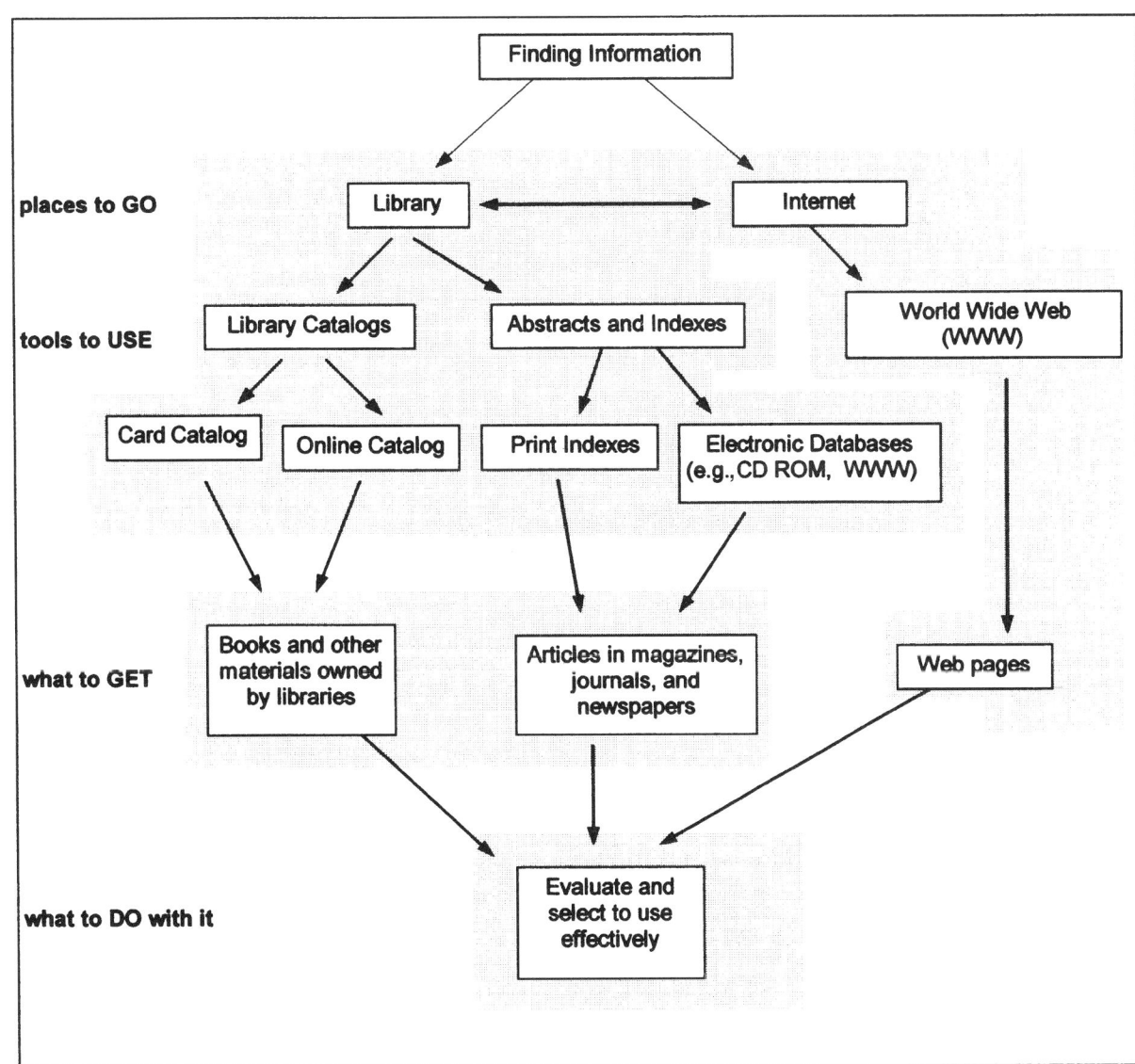

Copyright © 1999 by Allyn and Bacon.

1-1 *A Strategy for Using Information Literacy Skills (continued)*

The **library** is the first place you should go to find information. Your library has tools to use to identify materials found there. Your library also has tools to use to identify information in sources not owned by your library. Most of the tools you use in libraries are in electronic format, such as online catalogs and electronic databases. Your library may still have some important tools in print format, such as a card catalog and print indexes. In the library you can get books, magazines, journals, and other materials that contain information. Most of the books and other materials available in libraries are in print format, although materials such as newspaper and magazine articles increasingly are being made available in electronic format.

The **Internet** is another place you can go to find information. The Internet is a worldwide network of large computers. Information is available on computers connected to this network. The Internet allows you to use a personal computer to connect to and use information on this network. Anyone with access to the Internet can publish information on it.

The World Wide Web (**WWW**) is the most important tool to use to find information on the Internet. On the WWW you get web pages that contain information. However, most books, magazine, and journal articles are not yet available on the WWW. Databases for articles are beginning to be made available on the WWW, but they cost money. Many libraries are beginning to subscribe to these electronic databases on the WWW and make them available for their users.

Write a paragraph that summarizes your experiences in using the tools and resources in the library and on the Internet to find information.

Information Literacy and Research   1-2

Research is the process of inquiry and investigation in which you examine issues, probe topics, and ask questions. You will be doing research in your classes when you write papers, complete projects, and do class presentations.

Information literacy skills are necessary to conduct good research. Information literacy skills allow you to sift through the large amounts of information available in order to select the best information in support of your research.

Review your assigned papers, projects, and class presentations for the term. List those that will require you to use information literacy skills to do research.

Course/Class   *Assignment*   *Date Due*

Learning about Tools to Find Information   1-3

There are three major tools to **USE** to identify and locate information:

1. **Library Catalogs**: All libraries have a catalog that lists materials found in the library. The catalog describes each item and tells where it is located.

   Most libraries have an **online catalog** in which the information is entered into a computer. Libraries usually name their online catalogs. (e.g., LUIS, PELICAN, ORBIS)

   Some libraries also have a **card catalog** in which the information is typed on 3 × 5 cards and arranged alphabetically in file drawers. In these cases, the card catalog usually lists the older materials owned by the library. In some very large libraries, card catalogs may still be used for specific collections within the library (e.g., Government Documents, Special Collections.)

2. **Abstracts and Indexes**: These are sources used to identify citations in periodicals and newspapers. They are found in two formats:

   Print abstracts and indexes are available in many subject areas. Usually they are found in bound volumes. Each volume covers a certain period of time. Some print abstracts and indexes date from the nineteenth century.

   Electronic databases are available in many subject areas. Because this is a new technology, most databases include information only from 1960 to the present. Most databases include just a summary of the article, but some include the full text as well as a summary.

3. **World Wide Web**: The WWW is a popular way to explore the Internet. However, the WWW contains only a small portion of all information available in libraries. Books and most journal articles are not yet available on the WWW. Information on the WWW is organized on **web pages**. The first or top page in a set of web pages is called the **home page**. Anyone with access to the WWW can create a web page and publish information on the Internet.

Visit your library to learn about the major tools that are located there. Gather any handouts that will help you learn more about these tools. Ask the librarian if there are other instructional materials available to help you learn about these tools in your library (e.g., video, web tutorial).

Now answer these questions about tools in your library.

Learning about Tools to Find Information (continued) **1-3**

Library Catalogs

1. Does your library have an online catalog?

   If the online catalog has a name, write it here.

2. Can you connect to the online catalog from your home?

   Did you obtain information explaining how to do this?

3. What other interesting facts did you learn about your online catalog?

4. Does your library have one or more card catalogs?

5. If yes, what did you learn about the card catalogs in your library?

Abstracts and Indexes

6. Where are the print abstracts and indexes located in your library?

7. Did you find a list of databases owned by your library?

8. Write the name of one full-text database available in your library.

9. Can you connect to the databases from your home?

   Did you obtain information explaining how to do this?

World Wide Web

10. Can you use the World Wide Web on computers in your library?

11. Does your library have its own web pages?

Using a Card Catalog   1-4

A **card catalog** lists all the items found in the library. Information about each item is typed on a card and filed alphabetically in drawers. Each item has three cards to allow you to look for it in different ways. You can look for an item by subject, title, or author.

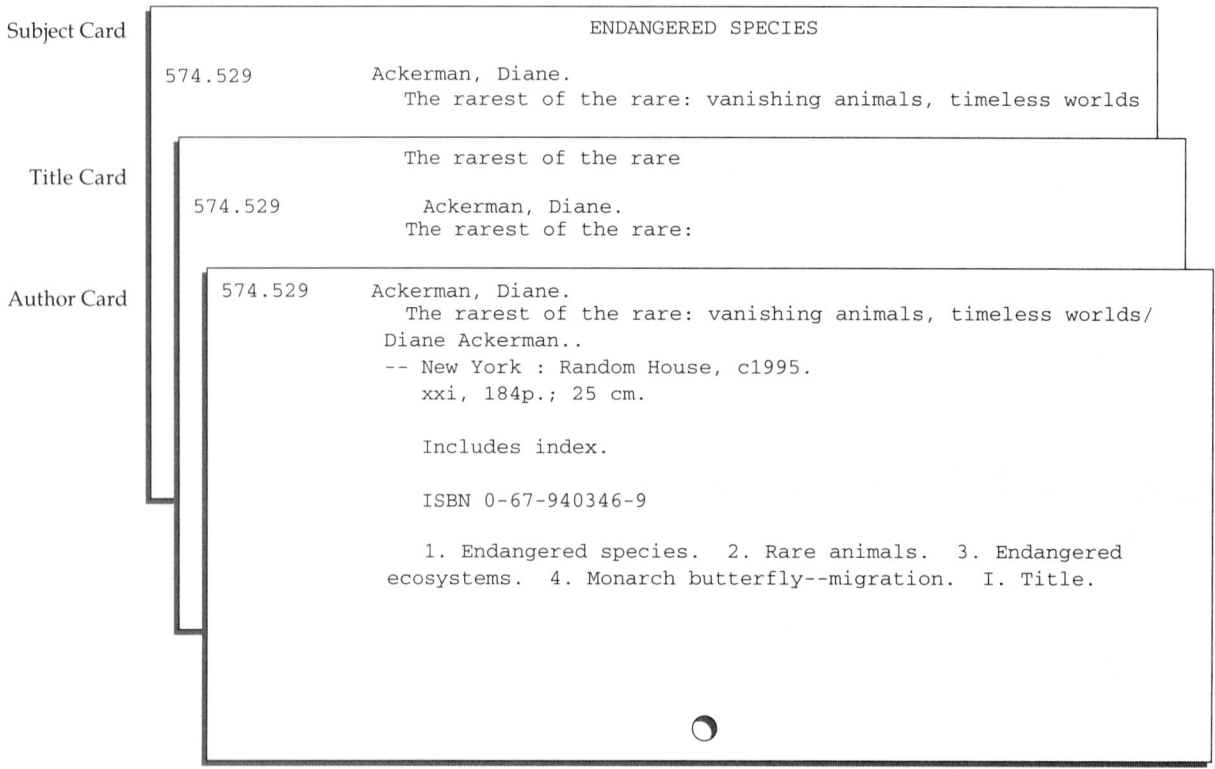

Look at the three cards and answer the questions:

1. What is the title of this book?

2. Who wrote it?

3. Under what subjects can you look to find this book?

4. When was this book published?

5. Who is the publisher?

6. How many pages are there?

Using an Online Catalog

1-5

Here is an example of a computer record in an **online catalog**. Whereas there are three types of cards for each item in a card catalog, there is only one computer record for each item in an online catalog. The information on a computer record is arranged in fields.

Fields   *Information in Each Field*

Author:	Cutlip, Glen W.
Title:	Learning and Information: skills for the secondary classroom and library media program/Glen W. Cutlip; edited by Paula Kay Montgomery.
Imprint:	Englewood, Colo.: Libraries Unlimited, 1988
Call number:	025.5
Physical features:	xvii, 134 p. : ill.; 28 cm.
Series:	Teaching library media research and information skills series
Notes:	Includes bibliography (p. 121–130) and index.
Other authors:	Montgomery, Paula Kay
Subjects:	Library orientation of high school students
	High school libraries
	Media programs (Education)
ISBN:	0872875806
OCLC no.	18987516

Use the example of a computer record from an online catalog to answer the questions:

1. Under what subjects could you find this book?

2. What is its title?

3. Who wrote it?

4. In what year was it published?

5. Who is the publisher?

6. How many pages are there?

7. Is there a bibliography?

8. Does the book have an index?

Using Your Online Catalog

1-6

Place a ✔ in front of each of the following that can be found using the online catalog in your library.

____ What years of a newspaper the library has.

____ If a book is checked out.

____ The latest issue of a magazine that the library received.

____ If a new book has been ordered.

____ Materials found in other libraries.

____ References to articles *in* magazines.

____ References to articles *in* newspapers.

____ The whole article from a magazine or newspaper or reference book.

Does your online catalog have a connection to:

____ a FreeNet?

____ the Internet?

If your library has a card catalog, describe how it is different from an online catalog.

Learning about Print Indexes and Electronic Databases

1-7

Indexes are used to locate articles in periodicals and newspapers. Periodicals, such as magazines, are published at regular intervals, sometimes weekly, sometimes monthly, and sometimes at other regular intervals throughout the year. Newspapers also are published at regular intervals, sometimes daily and sometimes weekly. Indexes help you locate articles on any topic in thousands of periodicals and newspapers. In addition to identifying articles about a topic, some indexes also include an **abstract**, or short summary, of an article.

Libraries own many indexes in **print** format. Print indexes look like books and are used to look up a topic. Each volume in an index covers a certain period of time. Usually an index covers a specific year. Some indexes date back as far as 1900.

1. What is the purpose of an index?

2. What is an abstract?

3. Are magazines periodicals?

4. How often are periodicals published?

5. How often are newspapers published?

Many libraries also own indexes in electronic formats. Electronic indexes are called **electronic databases**. In addition to including an abstract of an article, some electronic databases also include the entire article, or **full text**. Because electronic databases are a relatively new technology, many databases do not go back as far as print indexes. Databases are available in various electronic formats: CD ROM databases, online databases, and on the Internet.

6. What is another name for an electronic index?

7. Can you get the whole article on the computer if you use an electronic database?

8. If you want to find magazine articles for the year 1945, would you most likely use a print index or an electronic database?

9. What are the three electronic formats for databases?

Learning about Types of Print Indexes and Electronic Databases   1-8

Print indexes and electronic databases are tools to use to identify articles in periodicals and newspapers. The three major categories of indexes are **general, newspaper**, and **specialized**. There are many specific titles of indexes for each of these categories.

General print indexes and electronic databases cover a wide range of subjects and usually include popular magazines as well as selected scholarly journals. **Newspaper** print indexes and electronic databases cover one or more newspapers. **Specialized** print indexes and electronic databases cover specific disciplines such as psychology or education.

Most electronic databases have a print version. The print index may cover more years than the electronic database. Your library may also have some important print indexes that it does not have available as electronic databases.

Go to your library to locate electronic databases. Ask your librarian if there are lists or handouts that describe these. Then complete the following:

1. (a) The title of a **general** electronic database in my library is:

    (b) The dates this database covers are:

    (c) If there is a print version of this database, write its title and the dates it covers here:

2. (a) The title of a **newspaper** database in my library is:

    (b) The dates this database covers are:

    (c) If there is a print version of this database, write its title and the dates it covers here:

3. (a) The title of a **specialized** database for a specific discipline in my library is:

    (b) The dates this database covers are:

    (c) If there is a print version of this database, write its title and the dates it covers here:

Using Print Indexes and Electronic Databases

1-9

Print indexes provide citations to articles about a topic. A **citation** is the information that completely identifies a publication. The citation usually includes the author, title of the article, title of the publication, volume, issue, date of publication, and the page numbers. Often the titles of publications are abbreviated. The abbreviated titles are listed in the front of the index volume with their full titles.

Follow these steps when using a print index to locate information about a topic.

1. Look up a topic in the current volume.

2. Identify citations related to the topic.

3. If the title of a magazine or newspaper is abbreviated, look in the front of the index to find the complete title.

4. Check to see which magazines or newspapers included in the citations are available in your library.

Here is an example of a citation with its parts labeled:

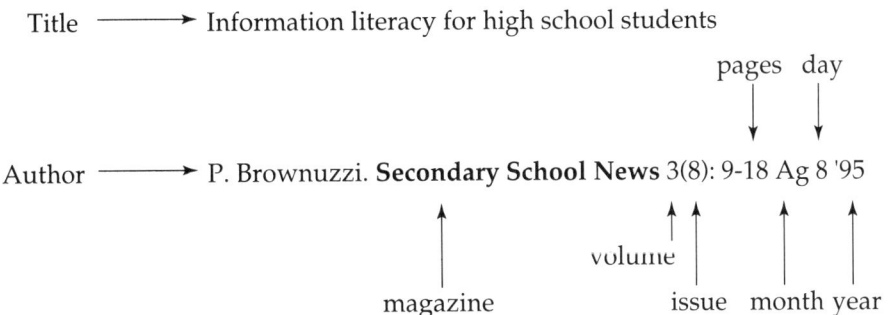

Here is another example. Label each part.

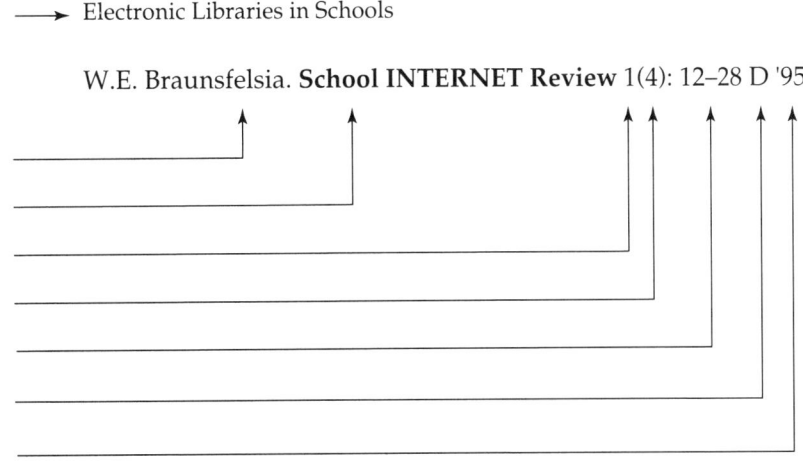

Copyright © 1999 by Allyn and Bacon.

19

1-9 *Using Print Indexes and Electronic Databases (continued)*

Electronic databases provide citations to articles about a topic. The citations contain all the information needed to find an article. In addition, the CD ROM database includes the abstract of an article and sometimes the full text as well. The information about each article is arranged in a record. There is one record for each article. Look at the sample record.

Sample CD ROM Record
From SIRS Researcher, SIRS, Inc., 1996

Volume:	SIRS 1995 Population, Volume Number 4, Article 3
Subject:	Keyword(s) : WATER and POLLUTION
Title:	Earth Is Running Out of Room
Author:	Lester R. Brown
Source:	USA Today (Magazine)
Publication Date:	Jan. 1995 Page Number(s): 30–32

Use the sample record to answer these questions:

1. What is the title of this article?

2. What magazine published this article?

3. When was the article published?

4. What is the name of the database used to locate this record?

5. What is the article about?

6. Who wrote the article?

7. How long is the article?

Learning about Keywords

1-10

You may need one or more keywords to do a computer search on a topic. A **keyword** is an important word about your topic. Because computers do exactly what you tell them to do, you will probably need more than one keyword to focus your search. If you ask the computer to search for the keyword *teenager*, it will find all the records with the keyword *teenager*. It will *not* find other forms of the keyword *teenager*, such as *teen* or *teenagers*. It will *not* find synonyms, such as *adolescent* or *adolescence*, or related terms such as *puberty*. Therefore, you should use more than one form of a keyword, such as its singular and plural forms, as well as synonyms and related terms for the keyword.

For the following topic, underline three words that can be used as keywords:

Using computers to manufacture cars

Write each keyword on the following chart. For each keyword, write other forms of the word as well as synonyms and related terms.

	1	2	3
Keywords			
Other Forms of Keyword			
Synonyms and Related Words			

Copyright © 1999 by Allyn and Bacon.

Learning about Boolean Connectors 1-11

Boolean connectors are used to search for information in online catalogs and electronic databases. The three Boolean connectors are the words **and**, **or**, and **not**. The diagrams illustrate the logic applied when a Boolean connector is used.

Connector	Use	Example	Diagram
and	Focus or narrow a search	computers and cars	◐
or	Expand or broaden a search	cars or automobiles	●●
not	Exclude specific terms	cars not trucks	◐

As shown below, connectors may be used more than once in the same search. When you use more than one **or** along with **and** in the same search, you must put parentheses around the concepts with **or**. The parentheses tell the computer to combine the records with **or** before combining the records with **and**.

The example shows how Boolean connectors are used to combine terms related to *cars* **and** *computers* **and** *manufacturing*. This search will retrieve computer records with the keywords *cars* **or** *automobiles* that also contain the keyword *manufacturing* **and** the keyword *computers*. Records containing the keyword *trucks* will *not* be retrieved.

Connectors	Example
or, and, and, not	(cars **or** automobiles) **and** manufacturing **and** computers **not** trucks

Use Boolean connectors to combine the following terms in a search for information about the effects of water pollution on animals. Use parentheses where appropriate. The combination of keywords and Boolean connectors is a **search statement**.

water   whales   pollution   oceans   ecology   dolphins   rivers   lakes   fish

Using Keywords and Boolean Connectors to Research Your Topic   1-12

1. Review your papers, projects, class presentations, and other assignments. Select one that requires you to do research and complete the following:

   I need to find information about the topic:

2. Underline words in your topic that you can use as keywords. Write these keywords on the chart. Write other forms of the keywords as well as synonyms and related terms.

	1	2	3
Keywords			
Other Forms of Keyword			
Synonyms and Related Words			

3. Use Boolean connectors to combine your keywords. Use parentheses where needed. Write your search statement here:

Learning about Truncation   1-13

How many words can you form using the base word *teach*? Write them here.

If you wanted to do a computer search of an online catalog or an electronic database to find all the words that can be formed beginning with the base word *teach*, you would need to use *truncation*. Look at the truncation that follows.

*teach**

The * is a *truncation symbol* that tells the computer to look for all forms of words that begin with the base word *teach*. Some databases use **?**, **!**, or **$** as truncation symbols. All have the same meaning as *.

Look at the truncated part of a word that follows and write all the forms of the word that can be made from it.

   1. *librar**

In this case, the * is a truncation symbol that tells the computer to look for all forms of words that begin with the part of the word *librar*.

Write the words that can be formed from each of the following truncations.

   2. *politic**

   3. *explor**

   4. *child**

   5. *immigra?*

   6. *govern$*

   7. *comput!*

Searching by Proximity   1-14

In a search strategy, you can specify that the keywords must be in **proximity** to each other. Here are three ways to search by keyword using proximity.

Adjacent Words

Use **adjacency** when you want the words to be next to each other. Here are examples of the most common ways to search for adjacent words:

    health adj care
    "health care"
    health (1w) care

In these examples, you will retrieve all records with *health* next to *care*.

Within a Paragraph

You can look for words within the same paragraph. Here are examples of the most common ways to search for keywords in the same paragraph.

    government **same** budget   government **with** budget
    government **near** budget   government **(5w)** budget

In these examples you will retrieve records with *government* in the same paragraph as *budget*.

Within a Specific Field

You can look for words within a **specific field** of a record. For example, here are common ways to search for a **k**eyword in a **t**itle field.

    astronaut **in ti**
    kt=astronaut
    astronaut:**ti**

In these examples, you will retrieve all records with *astronaut* in the title field.

1-14 *Searching by Proximity (continued)*

Complete the following to learn how to search by proximity in your online catalog or an electronic database. The help function provided by your online catalog or electronic database will help you complete this activity.

1. What is the name of the online catalog or electronic database you used?

2. If you selected an electronic database, does it have abstracts ____ or full text ____? (Check any that apply)

3. Can you search for words *adjacent* to each other? Yes ____ No ____

    If yes, write out a search statement that shows how to do it:

4. Can you search for words in the same paragraph? Yes ____ No ____

    If yes, write out a search statement that shows how to do it:

5. Write a search statement showing how to search for a word in the title field.

6. What else did you find out about proximity searching in this online catalog or electronic database?

Copyright © 1999 by Allyn and Bacon.

Learning about Controlled Vocabulary 1-15

All online catalogs and most electronic databases have **controlled vocabulary** for every record. Controlled vocabulary terms are specific terms assigned to each article as it is entered into the database. Controlled vocabulary tells what the article is about. Sometimes controlled vocabulary terms are called **subject headings** or **descriptors**. Some electronic databases have a thesaurus for all the terms used as controlled vocabulary. Sometimes the thesaurus is in print; sometimes it is electronic as a feature of the database. Here is an example of a record from an electronic database:

Search Request: K=ENDANGERED and ANIMAL?   **Wilson Biological and Agricultural Index**
Authors:
    Panou, Aliki
    Jacobs, Jurgen
    Panos, Dimitris.
Title:
    The endangered Mediterranean monk seal Monachus monachus in the Ionian Sea, Greece.
FOUND IN:
    Biological Conversation v. 64 no2 ('93) p. 129–40
Description:
    p. 129–40 : bibl il map.
Category(kn=):
    featu
Subject(s= or ks=):
    Wildlife conservation—Greece.
    Seals (Animals).
    Endangered species—Mammals.
ISSN (ns=):
    0006-3207

You can search this database by keywords. If you use any word in this record as a keyword, the computer will retrieve the sample record. The search strategy (endangered and animal?) retrieved this record. The subject headings for this record are listed under the field **Subjects**. These are controlled vocabulary terms/phrases that you can use to find information on that subject. The -- indicate a subheading. For example, *wildlife conservation* is a subject heading. -- *Greece* indicates that there are specific records with information about wildlife conservation limited to Greece. If you want *all* records about wildlife conservation, use just the main heading, *wildlife conservation*.

1. Would you retrieve this record if you used the search strategy: *endangered* **adj** *animal*?

    Explain your answer.

2. What are the subject headings assigned to this record?

3. What subject heading would have the most information about endangered animals?

Copyright © 1999 by Allyn and Bacon.

Using Controlled Vocabulary

1-16

Searching an online catalog or electronic database by controlled vocabulary is an efficient method of retrieving information. You will retrieve records specifically related to your topic and minimize the number of **false hits** that you retrieve. False hits are records that contain your keywords, but that are not on your subject.

For example, using the keywords *civil war* may retrieve records for articles about the war in Zaire, when you wanted articles about the civil war in the United States.

Follow these steps when searching an online catalog or electronic database:

1. Use keywords to search for your topic.
2. Select one record that is very close to or exactly on your topic.
3. Examine the record to find the subject headings or descriptors.
4. Repeat the search using the subject headings or descriptors listed.

Now use the online catalog in your library to apply these four steps.

1. Search for the keywords *family* and *violence*.

   How many records did you find?

2. Select one record that looks interesting and is on the topic.

   Write the title.

3. Examine the record to find the subject headings or descriptors.

   List the subject headings that are related to this topic?

4. Repeat the search using one of the subject headings or descriptors listed.

   How many records did you find?

5. Describe anything else you discovered about searching by subject heading instead of by keyword.

Copyright © 1999 by Allyn and Bacon.

Limiting by Date and Language   1-17

You may be able to limit your search to a specific year or range of years. You may also be able to limit your search to a specific language. Look for the word *limit* in your online catalog or electronic database to find instructions for how to limit your search by date or language.

Limit by Date

Here are examples of limiting a search by date. Look at each example and answer the question that follows it.:

1. 1980-1990   1980:1990

   Both will limit your results to records with publication dates from 1980 through 1990.

   What does *1972:1985* mean?

2. 1990–   >1990

   Both will limit your results to records with publication dates after 1990.

   What does *1972–* mean?

3. 199?

   This example uses truncation to limit your search by date to records with publications dates from 1990 through 1999.

   What does *197?* mean?

4. "Acid rain" and PY=1980–1990

   Some online catalogs and electronic databases use DT or DA for *date*, others use PY for *publication year*, and still others use YR for *year*. In this example, your search is limited to records with *acid* next to *rain* with publication dates from 1980 through 1990.

   What does the following search statement mean? *smoking and health and YR197?*

Copyright © 1999 by Allyn and Bacon.

1-17 Limiting by Date and Language (continued)

Limit by Language

Some online catalogs and electronic databases use LA or LG for *language*. Sometimes the languages are abbreviated and you must use the correct abbreviation according to the database. In some databases, you must use Boolean connectors to limit your search by language.

5. "acid rain" and LA:ger   acid adj rain and LA=ger

   In these examples, you will find records with *acid* next to *rain* written in German.

   What does the following search statement mean?

   "Desert Storm" and LA=Fre and DT=198?

Using Date and Language Limits

1-18

Complete the following to learn how to limit by date and by language in your online catalog or electronic database. The help function provided by your online catalog or electronic database will help you complete this activity.

1. What is the name of the online catalog or electronic database you used?

2. Write a search statement showing how to limit your search to records for titles published since 1995.

3. Write a search statement showing how to limit your search to records for titles published anytime in the 1980s.

4. Select a topic appropriate for your online catalog or electronic database. Write two keywords here:

   Now write a search statement showing how to limit your search to records with the keywords in the title and published between 1992 and 1996.

5. Write a search statement showing how to limit your search to records written in Spanish.

6. What else did you find out about limiting by date and by language in this online catalog or electronic database?

Copyright © 1999 by Allyn and Bacon.

Marking, Printing, Downloading, and Sending

1-19

When you do a search and find one or more records on your topic, you must:

1. Mark the records you decide to use.

2. Get the records you marked by:
   - printing them
   - downloading them to a disk
   - sending them to your e-mail address

Complete the following to learn how to mark, print, download, and send records in your online catalog or an electronic database. The "help" function provided by your online catalog or electronic database will help you complete this activity.

1. What is the name of the online catalog or electronic database you used?

2. Can you *mark* or *select* records in this database? Yes ____ No ____

   If yes, describe how to do it:

3. Describe how to print records:

4. Do you have to pay for printing?

5. Does the computer have its own printer, or is it networked?

6. Can you download records in this online catalog or electronic database? Yes ____ No ____

   If yes, describe how to do it:

7. Can you send records to your e-mail address in this online catalog or electronic database?

   Yes ____ No ____   If yes, describe how to do it:

Using Advanced Search Strategy Techniques

1-20

Follow these steps when looking for information in an online catalog or electronic database. Place a ✔ in front of each step when it is completed. Sign and date this checklist when the search strategy is completed. Submit it to your teacher with your completed assignment.

____ 1. Select a topic.

____ 2. Select keywords for your topic.

____ 3. Select other forms of the keyword and related terms.

____ 4. Use truncation as appropriate.

____ 5. Use Boolean connectors to create a search strategy.

____ 6. Do the search in the online catalog or electronic database(s) selected.

____ 7. Refine your search by selecting controlled vocabulary terms or descriptors.

____ 8. Limit by date and language as necessary.

____ 9. Select records to mark.

____ 10. Print, download, or send marked records to e-mail.

Answer Key

1-1 Paragraphs will vary.

1-2 Answers will vary.

1-3 Answers will vary.

1-4 1. The rarest of the rare: vanishing animals, timeless worlds. 2. Diane Ackerman. 3. Endangered Species; Rare animals; Endangered ecosystems, Monarch butterfly—migration. 4. 1995. 5. Random House. 6. 184.

1-5 1. Library orientation of high school students; High school libraries; Media programs (Education). 2. Learning and Information: skills for the secondary classroom and library media program. 3. Glen W. Cutlip. 4. 1988. 5. Libraries Unlimited. 6. 134. 7. yes. 8. yes.

1-6 Answers will vary.

1-7 1. To locate articles in periodicals and newspapers. 2. A short summary of an article. 3. yes. 4. At regular intervals, weekly, monthly, or at other regular intervals throughout the year. 5. At regular intervals, sometimes daily and sometimes weekly. 6. Electronic databases. 7. Sometimes. 8. Print index. 9. CD ROM, online, and on the Internet.

1-8 Answers will vary.

1-9 The citation should be labeled as follows:
title—Electronic Libraries in School
author—W. E. Braunsfelsia
magazine title—School INTERNET Review
volume—1
issue—4
pages 12–28
month—December
year—1995

1. Earth is running out of room. 2. USA Today. 3. January, 1995. 4. SIRS Researcher. 5. Water and pollution. 6. Lester R. Bown. 7. 3 pages.

1-10

	1	2	3
Keywords	computers	manufacture	cars
Other Forms of Keyword	computer computing	manufacturing manufacturer manufacturers	car
Synonyms and Related Words	automation technology robots	construct build produce	automobile automobiles vehicles

1-11 (whales or dolphins or fish) and (water or lakes or rivers or oceans) and (pollution or ecology)

ANSWER KEY

1-12 Answers will vary.

1-13 1. library, libraries, librarian, librarians, librarianship. 2. politics, political, politician, politicians. 3. explore, explores, explorer, explorers, exploring, explored, exploration. 4. child, children, childhood, childlike. 5. immigrant, immigrants, immigrate, immigration, immigrates. 6. government, governments, governs, governed, governing, governor, governors, governmental. 7. computing, compute, computes, computer, computers, computation.

1-14 Answers will vary.

1-15 1. No, because **endangered adj animal**? means that the words have to be next to each other, and they are not next to each other in this record. 2. Wildlife conservation—Greece; Seals (Animals); Endangered species—Mammals. 3. Endangered species.

1-16 Answers will vary.

1-17 1. Records limited to publication dates from 1972 through 1985. 2. Records limited to publication dates from 1972 to the present. 3. Records limited to publication dates from 1970 through 1979. 4. Records with the keyword *smoking* and the keyword *health* with publication dates from 1970 through 1979. 5. Records with the word *desert* next to the word *storm* written in French and with publication dates from 1980 through 1989.

1-18 Answers will vary.

1-19 Answers will vary.

1-20 Answers will vary.

CHAPTER TWO

Locating and Using Materials

CHAPTER OBJECTIVES

1. Teach students about the types and formats of materials found in a library.
2. Teach students how to locate library materials.

TITLES OF REPRODUCIBLE ACTIVITIES

2-1 Formats of Information
2-2 Types of Materials Found in a Library
2-3 Using Microforms
2-4 Learning about Call Numbers
2-5 Learning about the Dewey Decimal System
2-6 Learning about the Library of Congress System
2-7 Learning about Popular Magazines and Scholarly Journals
2-8 Using Popular Magazines and Scholarly Journals
2-9 Learning about Government Documents
2-10 Using Government Documents
2-11 Learning about Primary Sources
2-12 Using Primary Sources
Answer Key

USING THE REPRODUCIBLE ACTIVITIES

Use activities 2-1 through 2-3 to introduce students to the formats and types of materials found in a library. Use activities 2-4 through 2-6 to teach students about call numbers and classification systems used to locate library materials. Use activities 2-7 through 2-12 to teach students about specific library resources and where to find them in their library.

LOCATING AND USING MATERIALS **37**

2-1 Formats of Information

Explain that libraries have materials in different formats. Review the four formats of information with students. Describe the kind of equipment that may be needed to use information stored in each format. Then have students complete the activity.

You may extend this activity by showing students samples of each format.

2-2 Types of Materials Found in a Library

Describe each of the types of materials found in a library. Provide examples of each type where possible. Then have students complete the matching activity.

2-3 Using Microforms

Have students read the introductory text. You can extend this introduction by leading a class discussion about students' experiences using microforms. Then have students answer the questions about microforms found in their library.

2-4 Learning about Call Numbers

Have students read about call number systems and how they are used. Emphasize the importance of using call numbers to find the items within the library and on the shelves. Have students complete the activity

You can extend this activity by explaining to students the call number systems used by their school library, as well as by local libraries.

2-5 Learning about the Dewey Decimal System

Explain to students that the Dewey Decimal System is a numeric classification system used by most school and public libraries. Point out that most academic libraries use the Library of Congress system.

Review the ten major classes of the Dewey Decimal System with students. Explain to students that books on similar topics will be found near each other on the shelf. Define for students any terms they do not understand. Then have students complete 1 through 10.

Then use the example to show students that the Dewey Decimal System uses numbers that include decimals. The first line is a whole number and the second line is a decimal number. Point out that the call number $\frac{636}{.71}$ is the same as 636.71.

Review decimals as necessary. Explain how the call numbers in the example were placed in correct numerical order. Have students complete the Dewey Decimal ordering activity.

2-6 Learning about the Library of Congress System

Explain to students that the Library of Congress (LC) System is an alphanumeric classification system used by most academic libraries. Point out that most public libraries use the Dewey Decimal System.

Review the 20 major classes of the LC System with students. Explain to students that books on similar topics will be found near each other on the shelf. Define for students any terms they do not understand. Then have students complete 1 through 8.

Then use the example of call numbers to show students that the LC System uses numbers that include decimals. The first line is a whole number, and the second line starts with a decimal number. Point out that the call number JK560.R68 is the same as $\frac{JK}{560}$.

Review decimals as necessary. Explain how the call numbers in the example were placed in correct alphanumerical order. Have students complete the LC ordering activity.

2-7 Learning about Popular Magazines and Scholarly Journals

Use this activity to teach students the differences between popular magazines and scholarly journals. Emphasize that it is important to understand the differences between these periodical publications. Have students read the introductory text and complete the activity.

You may extend this activity by showing students sample issues of magazines and journals. Have students identify each title as popular or scholarly.

2-8 Using Popular Magazines and Scholarly Journals   [L]

Use this activity to have students apply what they learned in 2-7 about popular magazines and scholarly journals. Students will also need to apply skills they learned in Chapter One about using print indexes and electronic databases. Direct students to select a topic for which they need to find information. Have them use the library to complete the activity.

LOCATING AND USING MATERIALS **39**

2-9 Learning about Government Documents

Use this activity to teach students about documents published by local, state, federal, and international government bodies. Have students read about government documents. Use the examples to illustrate the creators of government documents. Have students use what they know about government bodies to complete the activity.

(Activity 5-13 teaches students to identify and use government publications on the WWW.)

2-10 Using Government Documents

Explain to students that most academic libraries and large public libraries have a Government Documents section. If your library is a Depository Library, you might want to explain what that term means. Have students complete this activity by going to their library and locating government documents. If they cannot browse the collections to find items in each category, they may need additional instruction in using the card or online catalog in their library to identify government documents.

2-11 Learning about Primary Sources

Have students read about primary sources. Use the examples to help them understand about the types of materials that are primary sources. Then have them complete the activity. You can also use this as a group activity where you provide the class with the events or place, and they brainstorm a list of possible primary sources.

2-12 Using Primary Sources

Explain to students that most academic libraries and large public libraries have a special section for original primary source materials. Have students read the introduction to learn about formats for primary source materials when the library does not own the original. Then have students go to the library to complete the activity and find one primary source. Tell students to use keywords such as *diary, correspondence, letters,* or *manuscript* in their search.

Formats of Information

2-1

Information in a library is packaged in many different ways. The way information is packaged is called a **format**. Four major formats are:

Print	Print format uses paper. Examples are books, magazines, newspapers, and pamphlets.
Electronic	Electronic formats use a computer to deliver information. Electronic formats include CD ROM and the Internet.
Audiovisual	Audiovisual (A/V) formats require you to watch or listen. Examples include slides, films, audio cassettes, and videocassettes.
Microform	Microforms reduce an image and put it on plastic to be read in a machine. Microfilm, microfiche, and microcartridge are examples of microforms.

Write the name of the format that goes with each illustration.

1.

2.

3.

4.

5.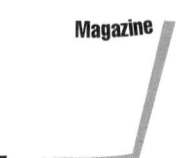

6.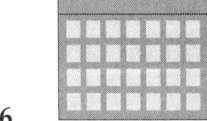

Copyright © 1999 by Allyn and Bacon.

Types of Materials Found in a Library

2-2

Many different types of materials are found in libraries. On the line in front of each type of material, write the letter corresponding to its description.

Material

Description

1. ____ government documents
2. ____ books
3. ____ magazines
4. ____ audio cassettes
5. ____ CD ROM
6. ____ microfiche
7. ____ journals
8. ____ reference books
9. ____ microfilm
10. ____ newspapers
11. ____ multimedia
12. ____ videocassette
13. ____ primary sources

A. Flat plastic cards, usually 4″ × 6″, with reduced images, read or copied on reader/printers.

B. A collection of articles written by experts in a specific field and published at regular intervals throughout the year, usually monthly or quarterly.

C. Materials to help you do research such as encyclopedias, almanacs, directories, and indexes. Usually these materials cannot be taken from the library.

D. Cartridge containing magnetic tape with a filmed or televised image, usually including sound, and viewed using a television monitor and VCR.

E. Small reels of plastic film that contain a reduced image, read or copied on reader/printers.

F. Small cartridge containing magnetic tape with recorded speech or sounds, and listened to using a tape recorder.

G. A daily publication containing news and opinions about current events, feature stories, and advertising.

H. Compact Disc Read Only Memory. A computer-based method of storing information as a database, requiring a computer and CD player for use.

I. Original sources of information such as diaries, letters, interviews, or photographs.

J. Materials published by local, state, federal, and international governments.

K. Extensive coverage of a subject printed on paper that is bound together in a single volume.

L. CD ROM database that uses full-text, video, sound, animation, color, and other features to provide information. Many reference books and encyclopedias are now available in this format.

M. A weekly or monthly publication, usually with glossy pictures and advertisements, containing articles written by journalists on topics of general interest.

Copyright © 1999 by Allyn and Bacon.

Using Microforms

2-3

In a microformat (**microform**), an image is reduced and put on plastic to be read in a machine. Microfilm, microfiche, and microcartridge are examples of microforms. Many library resources are available on microform. Books, magazines, newspapers, and even reference sources can be found on microform. For example, college catalogs from colleges around the world are available on microfiche. Microforms must be read and copied on special machines called reader/printers.

Libraries buy microforms for several reasons:

1. To save space (one 4" × 6" microfiche card can contain 200 pages of text)
2. To preserve materials that otherwise deteriorate over time (e.g., newspapers, magazines, original letters)
3. To acquire materials no longer available in their original form (e.g., very old books)

Answer the following questions about microforms in your library.

1. Does your library have a separate section for microforms? Yes ____ No ____

2. How many reader/printers does your library have?

3. What is the per page charge for making copies on the reader/printer?

4. Does your library have older newspapers on microfilm ____? on microfiche ____?

5. Does your library have older magazines on microfilm ____? on microfiche ____?

6. What else have you have learned about the kinds of materials available on microform in your library.

Learning about Call Numbers 2-4

When you locate items in a card or online catalog, the item will be identified by a **call number**. The call number tells the subject of the item and where it can be found on the library shelves. There are different systems of call numbers, but the three you must know about are the **Dewey Decimal System**, the **Library of Congress System**, and the **SuDocs (Superintendent of Documents) System**. Most school and public libraries use the Dewey Decimal System. Most academic and research libraries use the Library of Congress System. Government Documents collections in all libraries use the SuDocs System.

Call numbers in the three systems consist of a series of numbers or numbers and letters, and appear on the material. The three call number systems also use decimals. Some items may not be assigned a call number. If an item has a call number, it will be listed on the card in the card catalog, or on the record in the online catalog. When you write down a call number, be sure to note any **location** provided as well. The location may be a part of a library, or a branch library in the library system. You will not be able to find the item by its call number if you do not have the location that goes with it. For example, if the item is **Reference LB901.W6**, you must look in the reference area under that call number.

Here are examples of call numbers for the three systems:

    Dewey Decimal: 335.4309 (uses numbers and decimals)
    Library of Congress: LB1028.3 .K44 1996 (uses letters, numbers, and decimals)
    SuDocs: ED1.328/3:T23 (uses letters, numbers, decimals, dashes, slashes, and colons)

When you use a catalog, the call number may be written like this: LB45.C89 1997 but when you find the item on the shelf, it may be written like this:
  LB45
  .C89
  1997

Here are some sample call numbers. Next to each write the name of the system used.

    1. C13.2:T 22/7/996-2

    2. LB1050.46 .A84

    3. 975.938

    4. ED 1.310/2:211602

    5. N6538.N5 B43 1996

Learning about the Dewey Decimal System

2-5

Most school libraries are organized using the **Dewey Decimal System**. Books on similar subjects are grouped together under ten primary classes. The primary classes are represented by numbers. Here are the ten primary classes and the numbers that go with each.

000–099	Generalities	500–599	Pure Science
100–199	Philosophy and Related Areas	600–699	Technology (Applied Sciences)
200–299	Religion	700–799	The Arts
300–399	The Social Sciences	800–899	Literature and Rhetoric
400–499	Language	900–999	General Geography, History, etc.

Under which numbers would you find books on the following topics:

1. ____ the painter Van Gogh
2. ____ chemistry
3. ____ Catholic Church
4. ____ Spanish terms and expressions
5. ____ a general encyclopedia

6. ____ Countries that make up South America
7. ____ the Greek philosopher Aristotle
8. ____ the writer Mark Twain
9. ____ psychology
10. ____ using robots in industry

Call numbers in the Dewey Decimal System use numbers and decimals. The · on the second line is a decimal point. Look at these Dewey Decimal call numbers. They have been placed in correct numerical order.

11. Write the numbers 1–6 to show the correct numerical order of these call numbers.

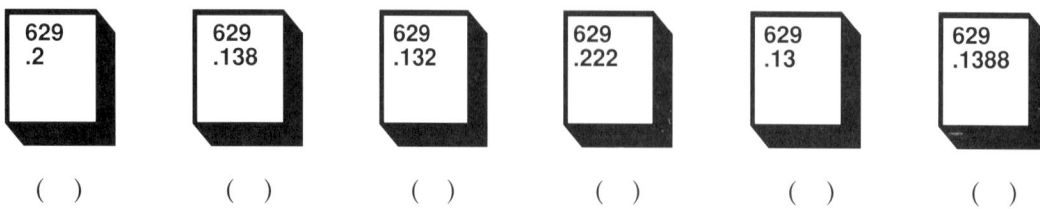

Learning about the Library of Congress System

2-6

The Library of Congress, located in Washington, D.C., is the largest library in the United States. The system developed to organize this library is called the **Library of Congress (LC) System**. The LC system is used in most academic libraries. Books on similar subjects are grouped together under 20 primary classes, which are represented by letters of the alphabet. Here are the 20 primary classes of the LC system and the letter(s) that goes with each.

General Works	A	Music	M
Philosophy, Psychology, Religion	B	Fine Arts	N
Archaeology, Genealogy, Biography	C	Language and Literature	P
History: General and Old World	D	Sciences	Q
History: Americas	E–F	Medicine	R
Geography, Anthropology, Recreation	G	Agriculture	S
Social Sciences	H	Technology	T
Political Sciences	J	Military Science	U
Law	K	Naval Science	V
Education	L	Bibliography, Library Science	Z

Under what letter would you find books on the following topics:

1. ____ King Henry VIII
2. ____ French novels
3. ____ Buddhism
4. ____ college guides
5. ____ football
6. ____ Michelangelo
7. ____ space shuttle
8. ____ cancer

Library of Congress call numbers are **alphanumeric**—that is, a series of numbers and letters. The • on the second line is a decimal point. Look at these Library of Congress call numbers. They tell the subject of the book and the place where the book belongs on the shelf. They have been placed in correct alphanumerical order.

9. Now write the numbers 1–5 to show the correct alphanumerical order of these call numbers.

( )   ( )   ( )   ( )   ( )

Copyright © 1999 by Allyn and Bacon.

Learning about Popular Magazines and Scholarly Journals

2-7

Many of your research projects will require you to find information in articles. Articles in popular magazines are very different from articles in scholarly journals. To evaluate the information you find, you must understand how articles in popular magazines differ from articles in scholarly journals.

Popular magazines include **recreational, news**, and **opinion** magazines. **Recreational magazines** are written for general entertainment. Examples of recreational magazines are: *People, Cosmopolitan*; and *Reader's Digest*. **News magazines** include general articles about current events and are written for the general public. Examples of news magazines are: *Time, Newsweek*, and *U.S. News and World Report*. **Opinion magazines** offer commentary about current events from a specific point of view. They are written for an educated audience but are not focused on an audience in a specific discipline. Examples of opinion magazines are: *The Nation, The New Republic*, and *National Review*.

Scholarly journals contain articles written by experts in a specific discipline. The articles present original research, reviews of research, or theoretical positions. Each discipline has its own scholarly journals. Examples of scholarly journals are: *JAMA: Journal of the American Medical Association, Journal of Educational Psychology*, and *Journal of the Academy of Marketing Science*.

Here are characteristics of popular magazines and scholarly journals. Write **P** in front of each characteristic you think describes articles found in popular magazines and **S** for each that describes articles found in scholarly journals.

1. ____ are specialized for a specific discipline.

2. ____ do *not* include footnotes or a bibliography of sources.

3. ____ usually include glossy pages, many pictures, and advertisements.

4. ____ are written by scholars in the discipline.

5. ____ do not include original research, but may include stories about the research.

6. ____ use terminology of a discipline.

7. ____ are written by journalists.

8. ____ have few glossy pictures and usually no advertisements.

9. ____ are often published by a professional organization.

10. ____ cite sources in footnotes or a bibliography.

Using Popular Magazines and Scholarly Journals   2-8

Review the papers, projects, and class presentations you must do this semester. Select one that requires you to do research, and complete the following:

I need to find information about the topic:

Complete the following activity for both a **popular magazine** and a **scholarly journal**.

Popular Magazine

1. Use an electronic database or a print abstract and index to identify an article about your topic found in a popular magazine. Write the complete citation.

2. Find the article in your library. Write its location and call number (if there is one).

3. Read the article and identify three things you learned about your topic.

Scholarly Journal

4. Use an electronic database or a print abstract and index to identify an article about your topic found in a scholarly journal. Write the complete citation.

5. Find the article in your library. Write its location and call number (if there is one).

6. Read the article and identify three things you learned about your topic.

7. In what ways are scholarly journal articles different from articles in popular magazines?

Copyright © 1999 by Allyn and Bacon.

Learning about Government Documents **2-9**

Government documents are materials published by local, state, federal, or international governments. Government documents cover all subject areas. They are published in all formats (e.g., microfiche, CD ROM) and include all types of resources (e.g., magazines, maps).

The Government Documents section of your library may have its own tools such as a card catalog or electronic database. Many government databases are on CD ROM. A large amount of government information is also available on the WWW. Your library may have one or more government document librarians to help you locate and use government documents.

Local documents are published by any agency or organization that is part of a city, municipality, or county government. Creators of local documents include the school board, the zoning commission, and the town clerk.

    1. Write the name of another creator of local documents:

State documents are published by any agency or organization that is part of a state government. Creators of state documents include the legislature, the Board of Regents, and the Bureau of Prisons.

    2. Write the name of another creator of state documents:

Federal documents are published by any agency or organization that is part of the U.S. government. Creators of federal information include the U.S. Congress, the National Park Service, the Armed Forces, the Department of Commerce, and the Environmental Protection Agency.

    3. Write the name of another creator of federal documents:

International documents are published by any agency or organization that is part of the government of another country, or by any multinational organization formed by several governments. Creators of international documents include the United Nations (UN) the Organization of American States (OAS), and the North Atlantic Treaty Organization (NATO).

    4. Write the name of another creator of international documents:

Using Government Documents

2-10

Visit your library to answer the following questions:

1. Does your library have a separate Government Documents section?

2. If yes, is there a desk or service point where you can get help?

3. If no, where are government documents located in your library?

4. Find one document for each of the following categories. For each document write the author, title, and call number as it appears in your card or online catalog.

Local Document

Author:

Title:

Call Number:

State Document

Author:

Title:

Call Number:

Federal Document

Author:

Title:

Call Number:

International Document

Author:

Title:

Call Number:

Learning about Primary Sources 2-11

Primary sources are original sources of information from people who had first-hand experience with an event. Primary sources include: interviews, diaries, journals, photographs, architectural drawings, letters or other correspondence, and sometimes even newspaper accounts. Primary sources provide an interesting "I was there" perspective.

Examples of primary sources are the following:

- Diary of a woman who traveled west in a covered wagon
- Letters from a soldier in the Civil War
- Correspondence between the president of the United States and the leader of another country
- Video interview with the survivor of a concentration camp
- Journal of a child who survived the sinking of the Titanic
- Photographs of the construction of the Empire State Building
- First draft of the manuscript for *Huckleberry Finn*
- Blueprints for your school
- Newspaper article written the day the Japanese bombed Pearl Harbor

1. Select an event in history. Then list two items that would be primary sources about that event.

   Event:

   Primary sources:

2. Select another event. List two items that would be primary sources about that event.

   Event:

   Primary sources:

3. Select a place. Now list two items that would be primary sources about that place.

   Place:

   Primary sources:

Copyright © 1999 by Allyn and Bacon.

Using Primary Sources

2-12

Primary sources are often original documents created at a specific point in time. But libraries may also own published, microform, or electronic versions of the original documents. These are also primary sources. Academic libraries and many large public libraries have a special department with primary sources, often called Special Collections, Manuscripts, or Archives.

1. Does your library have a section or department for primary sources? Yes ____ No ____

    If yes, what is the name of this section/department?

    Does this section have its own catalog or do you use the library card or online catalog to identify primary sources?

2. Use your library catalog to find a published version of a primary source. Write the title and call number for one primary source in your library.

    Title:

    Call number:

3. Locate the item and describe it. Explain why it is a primary source.

Answer Key

2-1 1. Audiovisual. 2. Electronic. 3. Print. 4. Audiovisual. 5. Print. 6. Microform.
2-2 1. J 2. K 3. M 4. F 5. H 6. A 7. B 8. C 9. E 10. G 11. L 12. D 13. I
2-3 Answers will vary.
2-4 1. SuDocs. 2. Library of Congress. 3. Dewey Decimal. 4. SuDocs. 5. Library of Congress.
2-5 1. 700-799. 2. 500-599. 3. 200-299. 4. 400-499. 5. 000-099. 6. 900-999. 7. 100-199. 8. 800-899. 9. 300-399. 10. 600-699. 11. (5) (3) (2) (6) (1) (4)
2-6 1. D 2. P 3. B 4. L 5. G 6. N 7. T 8. R 9. (3) (5) (2) (4) (1)
2-7 1. S 2. P 3. P 4. S 5. P 6. S 7. P 8. S 9. S 10. S
2-8 1 through 6 answers will vary. 7. Answers should reflect what was learned in activity 2-7.
2-9 Answers will vary.
2-10 Answers will vary.
2-11 Answers will vary.
2-12 Answers will vary.

CHAPTER THREE

Using Reference Sources

CHAPTER OBJECTIVES

1. Teach students about reference sources available in both print and electronic formats.
2. Teach students how to locate and use basic reference sources.

TITLES OF REPRODUCIBLE ACTIVITIES

3-1 Learning about Reference Sources
3-2 Learning about Electronic Reference Sources
3-3 Locating Print and Electronic Dictionaries
3-4 Using a Dictionary
3-5 Comparing Information from Dictionaries
3-6 Locating Print and Electronic Encyclopedias
3-7 Using a Print Encyclopedia
3-8 Comparing Information from Print Encyclopedias
3-9 Using a Multimedia Encyclopedia
3-10 Comparing Information from Print and Multimedia Encyclopedias
3-11 Locating Almanacs
3-12 Using Almanacs
3-13 Locating Statistical Sources
3-14 Using Statistical Abstract of the United States
3-15 Locating Print and Electronic Atlases
3-16 Using Print Atlases
3-17 Using Electronic Atlases
3-18 Locating Biographical Sources
3-19 Using Biographical Sources
3-20 Locating Chronologies
3-21 Using Chronologies
3-22 Locating Reference Sources for Literary Criticism
3-23 Using Reference Sources for Literary Criticism
3-24 Using Reference Sources
Answer Key

USING THE REPRODUCIBLE ACTIVITIES

Use activities 3-1 and 3-2 to introduce students to the different types and formats of reference sources in both print and electronic formats. Activities 3-3 through 3-23 provide specific instruction and activities for each of the types of reference sources covered in the overview in 3-1. Use activity 3-24 to have students apply what they have learned about all the types of print and electronic reference sources.

3-1 Learning about Reference Sources

Explain to students that reference sources are authoritative sources for factual information. They have a reputation for using experts to compile and write the information provided, and their standards for quality control are rigorous. Have students read about the most frequently used types of reference sources. Then have students answer the questions.

You can extend this activity by asking students to share their experiences using reference sources.

3-2 Learning about Electronic Reference Sources

Use this activity to introduce students to the concept that reference sources are beginning to be made available in various electronic formats. Explain that some reference sources are published on CD ROM or on the Internet via the WWW. Have students read the introduction and answer the questions. Define *multimedia* for students who are unfamiliar with the term.

Ask students to share their experiences using electronic reference sources. Point out that in many cases the electronic versions offer additional features, such as the ability to search by keywords using Boolean connectors; hyperlinked words, phrases, and images to click on and jump to related information; and multimedia applications such as audio, video, and animation.

3-3 Locating Print and Electronic Dictionaries [L]

Have students read about the different types of dictionaries. Then have students complete the activity by using the library to find examples of each type of dictionary, in either print or electronic format. Remind students to use the online or card catalog to locate dictionaries in the library. Provide assistance as necessary.

USING REFERENCE SOURCES **55**

3-4 Using a Dictionary

Have students read about the different types of information found on a dictionary page. Explain any terms they do not understand. Point out that there may be variations between dictionaries but that the basic information on the page remains the same. Then have students complete the activity.

3-5 Comparing Information from Dictionaries

Tell students that they may need to use different types of dictionaries to find information about a word. Review what students have learned about dictionaries in 3-3. Have them look up the meaning of the word *radical*. This word was chosen because it has many different meanings. Have students complete the activity by writing the first definition of the word *radical* from each of the four types of dictionaries. Ask students to share how the definitions they found differed.

3-6 Locating Print and Electronic Encyclopedias

Have students read about the different types of encyclopedias. Tell them that encyclopedias constitute a large part of a reference collection in a library and that they have reputations for accuracy, expertise, and currency. Explain to students that electronic encyclopedias may be on CD ROM, such as the multimedia encyclopedias frequently sold with new computers, or may be available on the Internet.

Then have students complete the activity by using the library to find examples of each type of encyclopedia in either print or electronic format. Remind students to use the online or card catalog to locate encyclopedias in the library. Provide assistance as necessary.

3-7 Using a Print Encyclopedia

Tell students that a keyword and index are used to locate information about a topic in a print encyclopedia. For example, a student looking for information about *cars* might go to the C volume but may not find an entry for *cars*. However, if the student looks for *cars* in the index volume, the entry for *cars* will provide a cross reference to the A volume for *automobiles*, or the T volume for *transportation*. Use the sample index entry to explain the types of information found in an encyclopedia index entry. Then have students look at the sample entry for "Rap music" and answer the questions.

3-8 Comparing Information from Print Encyclopedias [L]

Review with students the differences between general and subject encyclopedias from 3–6. Use this activity to have students compare the kind of information they will find when they look up the same topic in two different kinds of print encyclopedias. You may either provide the names of two specific encyclopedias for students to use, or ask them to identify encyclopedias on their own. Have students go to the library to complete the activity.

3-9 Using a Multimedia Encyclopedia [C]

Use this activity only if the students have access to a multimedia encyclopedia.

Explain to students that multimedia encyclopedias on CD ROM are very common. Many are included with the purchase of a new computer. Point out that basic computer skills are needed to use a multimedia encyclopedia successfully. These skills include: keyboard/mouse skills; scrolling; using navigation buttons; and, some familiarity with tool/task bars and pop-up windows.

Have students read the introductory text about icons. Use the examples to explain the various functions. Tell students that depending on the multimedia encyclopedia used, not all icons may be found, or they may look different. Then have students use a multimedia encyclopedia to find information about Haiti. Have students answer the questions using a multimedia encyclopedia.

3-10 Comparing Information from Print and Multimedia Encyclopedias
[L] [C]

Review the differences between print and multimedia encyclopedias. Have students complete the activity by looking up the same topic in both types of encyclopedias and describing their experiences. You may provide the names of encyclopedias to use or ask the students to identify two titles on their own. Then lead students in a discussion about how they compared the two encyclopedias. You may extend this activity by asking students to share their experiences using encyclopedias in print and multimedia format.

3-11 Locating Almanacs [L]

Have students read about almanacs. Then have students complete the activity by using the library to find each almanac listed. Remind students to use the online or card catalog to look up the title of each almanac to find its location and call number.

3-12 Using Almanacs [L]

Review the introductory text with students. Tell them they should use the index to find facts in an almanac. Caution students that depending on the almanac they use, the index may be in the front, middle, or back. Have students locate almanacs in the library to complete the activity. Tell them to use the current edition. You can use this activity as a group project, or as a competition between individuals and/or groups. Later, have students share their experiences in using almanacs to locate facts.

3-13 Locating Statistical Sources [L]

Have students read about statistical sources. Point out the differences between general and specialized statistical sources. Remind students to use the online or card catalog to look up the title of each source to find its location and call number. Help students use the card or online catalog to identify the statistical abstract for their state, as well as a statistics source on a specific topic. Then have students complete the activity by using the library to find the statistical sources.

3-14 Using Statistical Abstract of the United States [L]

Use this activity to have students use the *Statistical Abstract of the United States*. Review the introductory text and the steps with students. Have students follow the steps to answer the three questions and provide the required information.

You can use this activity as a group project or as a competition between individuals and/or groups. Later, have students share their experiences using this statistical source.

Activities 4–1 through 4–3 provide tables from the *Statistical Abstract of the United States*. You may wish to include these activities here.

3-15 Locating Print and Electronic Atlases [L]

Have students read about the different types of atlases. Explain to students that electronic atlases may be on multimedia such as CD ROM, or they may be available on the Internet. Then have students complete the activity by using the library to find examples of each type of atlas in either print or electronic format. Remind students to use the online or card catalog to locate atlases in the library. Provide assistance as necessary.

3-16 Using Print Atlases   [L]

Review the introductory text with students. Emphasize that students may have to use more than one type of atlas to answer the questions. Have students locate atlases to complete the activity. Help students use the card or online catalog to identify atlases to complete the activity.

You can use this activity as a group project, or as a competition between individuals and/or groups. Later, have students share their experiences in using atlases to locate information.

Activities 4-10 and 4-11 provide maps. You may wish to include those activities here.

3-17 Using Electronic Atlases   [C]

Use this activity only if your students have access to an electronic atlas or to the WWW.

Review the introductory text with students. Then have them use an electronic atlas to find information about Sudan. Have students answer the questions about the information they found. Then lead a discussion about the differences between print and multimedia atlases. Ask students to share their experiences using an electronic atlas.

3-18 Locating Biographical Sources   [L]

Explain to students why they will need to use biographical sources. Tell them that when they need information about a person, an entire book about the person may provide more information than they need, while an encyclopedia may provide little or no information about that person. In either case, students should use biographical sources. Direct students to read the introductory text and complete the activity. Remind students to use the online or card catalog to look up the title of each biographical source to find its location and call number.

You may need to help students locate specialized biographical sources in their library. Explain how they can use the card or online catalog to find specialized biographical sources.

Finally, you may need to tell your students the name of any electronic biographical source available in their library.

3-19 Using Biographical Sources [L]

Have students use biographical sources to locate information about each person listed. Remind students that they may need to look in more than one source to find the person listed.

You can use this activity as a group project or as a competition between individuals and/or groups. Later, have students share their experiences in using biographical sources to locate information.

3-20 Locating Chronologies [L]

Explain to students that chronologies present information organized by date. Direct students to read the introductory text and complete the activity. Remind students to use the online or card catalog to look up the title of each chronology to find its location and call number.

You may need to help students locate a specialized chronology in their library. Explain how they can use the card or online catalog to find a specialized chronology.

3-21 Using Chronologies [L]

Have students use the chronologies they located in the library to answer the questions. Remind students that they may need to look in more than one source to find the information needed.

You can use this activity as a group project or as a competition between individuals and/or groups. Later, have students share their experiences in using chronologies to locate information.

3-22 Locating Reference Sources for Literary Criticism [L]

Explain to students that sources for literary criticism are a good place to start to look for criticism of an author's works. Direct students to read the introductory text and complete the activity. Remind students to use the online or card catalog to look up the title of each source of literary criticism to find its location and call number. Substitute or add other titles if your library has other important sources.

If your library does not own the Dictionary of Literary Biography, substitute another title that includes both literary criticism and biographical information.

Finally, you may need to tell your students the name of any electronic source for literary criticism available in their library.

3-23 Using Reference Sources for Literary Criticism

Have students use the reference sources for literary criticism they located to identify three major themes in an author's work. Have students compare the themes they found in the works of the various authors.

You may alter or extend this activity by providing the names of other authors.

3-24 Using Reference Sources

Use this activity to have students apply what they have learned about the various types of reference sources. Have students complete the activity by writing the type of reference source that could be used to answer the question. There may be more than one appropriate source.

Learning about Reference Sources   3-1

Reference sources are used to find information on a topic quickly. The most frequently used reference sources are dictionaries, encyclopedias, almanacs, statistical sources, atlases, biographical sources, chronologies, and sources for literary criticism. Some reference sources are available in electronic format. Read about the different types of reference sources. Then answer the questions.

A **dictionary** provides information about words. **Unabridged dictionaries** attempt to include all words currently in use in a language. **Abridged dictionaries** are shortened forms of unabridged dictionaries in which infrequently used words are omitted. **Etymological dictionaries** tell the history of words and explain how their meaning has changed over time. **Subject dictionaries** are found for many specific subjects, such as medicine, psychology, art, music, business, science, or technology. Subject dictionaries provide longer or more technical definitions of the terms and concepts for a discipline than do other types of dictionaries.

An **encyclopedia** contains articles on a variety of subjects written by experts. The articles are arranged in alphabetical order by topic. **General encyclopedias** include overview articles on a wide range of topics. **Single-volume encyclopedias** include short articles arranged in alphabetical order. **Foreign language encyclopedias** may be in a foreign language, or about a foreign country, or both. **Subject encyclopedias** are found for many specific subjects, such as science, art, or music. The articles are longer, more complete, and more technical than those found in general encyclopedias.

An **almanac** is a single-volume reference book containing facts, data, tables, charts, lists, and other methods of organizing useful information. Some almanacs are for a specific subject.

A **statistical source** contains statistics on different topics. Many statistical sources include abstracts or summaries of data from longer reports. **General statistical sources** include statistics on many topics. **Specialized statistical sources** include statistics on a specific topic.

An **atlas** is a collection of maps. A **general world atlas** contains maps showing physical and political features of countries throughout the world. **Historical atlases** contain maps that portray an event or show how something developed over a period of time. Historical atlases include information about topics such as changes in borders, military campaigns, exploration, or culture. **Subject atlases** contain maps related to a specific place or topic.

Biographical sources provide concise background information about the lives and accomplishments of famous people, living or dead. These sources are useful if you do not need or cannot find an entire book about a person.

A **chronology** is a reference book that presents information organized by date. Chronologies may cover events over a long time, such as hundreds of years, or as short a time as one year. Some chronologies cover all subjects while other chronologies cover specific subjects.

Sources for literary criticism contain overview articles about authors and their works. They provide condensed criticism of an author's work. They often include information extracted from articles in magazines and journals. Some sources for literary criticism are **biographical**, focusing on

Copyright © 1999 by Allyn and Bacon.

61

3-1 *Learning about Reference Sources (continued)*

the author's life with a summary of his or her work. Other literary criticism sources focus on **genre** (such as poetry or drama), **country** (such as English literature or German literature), or **period** (such as the eighteenth century).

1. Where should you look to find the most complete definition of a technical word?

2. What is the difference between a general encyclopedia and a subject encyclopedia?

3. What reference sources would you use to find data?

4. What kind of dictionary includes almost every word that people use today?

5. What kind of reference source arranges information by date?

6. What is a collection of maps bound together as a book called?

7. What is an abridged dictionary?

8. When would you use a biographical source?

9. What would you use to find criticism of an author's work?

10. When would you use a historical atlas?

11. Which type of encyclopedia includes articles on a wide variety of topics?

12. What are foreign language encyclopedias?

13. What does a subject atlas contain?

Learning about Electronic Reference Sources

3-2

Many reference sources are now available in electronic formats. A common electronic format for reference sources is **CD ROM**. Some CD ROM reference sources are **multimedia**. They are called multimedia because they contain images, sound, video, and animation. Other CD ROM reference sources are **text-only**. This means they contain only the text without images, sound, video, and animation. Another electronic format for reference sources is the **Internet**. Some electronic reference sources on the Internet are text-only; others are multimedia.

1. Describe any electronic reference sources you have used.

2. Think about a time when you used a print reference source to find information. Describe the type of reference source you used and what information you found.

3. Now think about multimedia. Imagine that the information in the print reference source was available on a multimedia CD ROM. Describe how the information would be presented differently.

Copyright © 1999 by Allyn and Bacon.

Locating Print and Electronic Dictionaries   3-3

Dictionaries are reference books that provide information about words. Dictionaries help you pronounce a word, discover its meaning, and learn how it is spelled. Dictionaries are made up of entries. An **entry** is a word, abbreviation, prefix, suffix, or word part that is listed and defined in the dictionary. Dictionaries are available in both print and electronic form.

There are five basic types of dictionaries. Each has its own value. Knowing about the different types will help you decide when to use each.

Unabridged Dictionaries. *Unabridged* means not condensed or shortened. Unabridged dictionaries attempt to include all words currently in use in a language. An example of an unabridged dictionary is the *Random House Dictionary of the English Language*.

Abridged Dictionaries. *Abridged* means shortened by the omission of something. Abridged dictionaries are shortened forms of unabridged dictionaries. Abridged dictionaries omit words that are not frequently used. They are smaller, lighter, and less expensive than abridged dictionaries. An example of an abridged dictionary is the *American Heritage Dictionary*.

Etymological Dictionaries. *Etymology* is the history of words. Etymological dictionaries tell the history of words and explain how their meaning has changed over time. Etymological dictionaries can be one or more volumes. An example of an etymological dictionary is the *Oxford English Dictionary*.

Slang Dictionaries. *Slang* is used mostly for casual speech. An example of slang is *def*. The slang meaning of this expression is "excellent," as in *def jam*, which means "great music." An example of a slang dictionary is the *Oxford Dictionary of Modern Slang*.

Subject Dictionaries. Special dictionaries are found for many subjects, such as medicine, psychology, art, music, business, science, and technology. An unabridged dictionary will probably provide a definition for a technical word in a given subject. However, if a special dictionary exists for that subject, a longer or more complete definition will be found in the subject dictionary. An example of a subject dictionary is *Stedman's Medical Dictionary*.

Locating Print and Electronic Dictionaries (continued) **3-3**

Now find another example of each of type of dictionary. Write its title and call number. Include a location with the call number if provided. Then ✔ *Print* or *Electronic* to show the format of the dictionary.

Unabridged Dictionary

Title

Call number   Print _____   Electronic _____

Abridged Dictionary

Title

Call number   Print _____   Electronic _____

Etymological Dictionary

Title

Call number   Print _____   Electronic _____

Slang Dictionary

Title

Call number   Print _____   Electronic _____

Subject Dictionary

Title

Call number   Print _____   Electronic _____

CORETTE LIBRARY CARROLL COLLEGE

Copyright © 1999 by Allyn and Bacon.

Using a Dictionary

3-4

Read about the types of information you will find on a dictionary page. Refer to this information to complete the activity.

1. **Guide words.** There are two guide words at the top of every page in a dictionary. The first guide word is called the *opening guide word*. It shows the first word on the page. The second guide word is called the *closing guide word*. It shows the last word on the page.

2. **Entry words.** Entry words are the words listed and defined on the page. They are in bold type to make them easy to locate.

3. **Phonetic respellings.** Each entry word is followed by a respelling, usually in parentheses. The respelling uses symbols and different letters that help you pronounce the word. The *short pronunciation key* usually found at the bottom of the page shows you what the symbols and letters mean.

4. **Part of speech.** Usually after the respelling you will find an abbreviation that tells the part of speech for the entry word. The abbreviation is often in italics. Here are the abbreviations for the common parts of speech:

   n = noun   *v* = verb   *adj* = adjective
   pron = pronoun   *adv* = adverb   *prep* = preposition

5. **Definitions.** The definitions for each entry word are included. The definitions are numbered to show their common use. The most common definition is listed as **1.** The next most common definition follows **2.** and so on.

6. **Variants of the word.** The entry word may also include different forms of the word. For example, *directed, directing,* and *directs* may be included with the entry word *direct*.

7. **Origin or etymology.** Some dictionaries will include information that tells the language that the word came from. Sometimes this information is in brackets [ ]. In some cases, an abbreviation for the original language may be included, such as **G** for Greek and **L** for Latin. Some dictionaries will also provide the original word and its definition.

8. **Usage.** Sometimes an entry contains information about how to use the word properly. Most often, a sentence containing the entry word is provided to show how the word might be used in a sentence.

9. **Synonym or antonym.** Sometimes synonyms and/or antonyms for the entry word are provided. The abbreviation *syn* is used to show the synonyms. The abbreviation *ant* is used to show the antonyms.

10. **Illustration.** Sometimes drawings or photographs are included to illustrate the entry word.

11. **Short pronunciation key.** This key to the pronunciation of words is usually found at the bottom of every dictionary page. The short pronunciation key contains letters, numbers, symbols, and words that will help you pronounce words correctly. If the short pronunciation key does not help you pronounce an entry word, then look at the *long pronunciation key* at the front of your dictionary.

Using a Dictionary (continued) 3-4

Here is a sample entry from a dictionary. Each part of the entry that provides a type of information is numbered. Refer to the numbered list on page 66 of the types of information found on a dictionary page. Identify each type of information by placing a number in the box near the information provided.

☐ glitter

☐ gloss

☐ **globe.** (glōb) ☐ *n.* ☐ **1.** Any body having the shape of a ☐ sphere; especially, a representation of the earth or heavens in the shape of a hollow ball. **2. a.** The earth itself. Usually used with *the.* b. Any planet. **3.** Any object resembling a globe; especially a rounded container, such as a fishbowl or a protective or decorative covering for a light bulb. -*v.* **globed, globing, globes.**

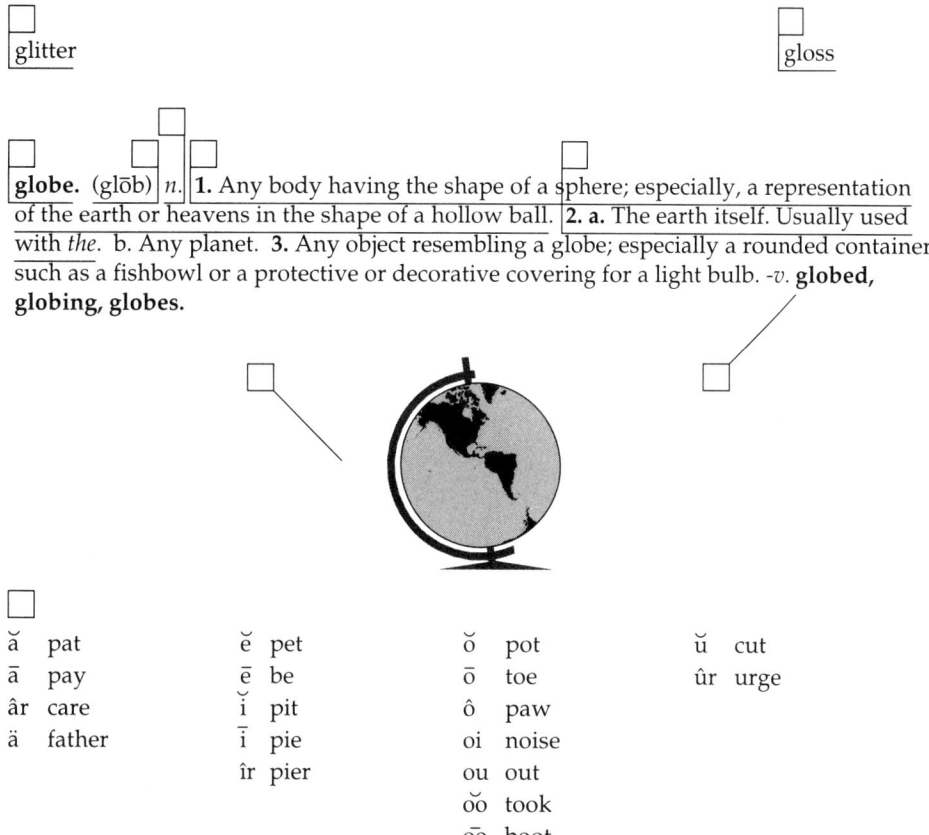

☐

ă pat	ĕ pet	ŏ pot	ŭ cut
ā pay	ē be	ō toe	ûr urge
âr care	ĭ pit	ô paw	
ä father	ī pie	oi noise	
	îr pier	ou out	
		ŏŏ took	
		ōō boot	

Comparing Information from Dictionaries   3-5

Different types of dictionaries provide different kinds of information about a word. Look up the word *radical* in the following four types of dictionaries. Write the first definition you find for each.

1. Abridged:

2. Etymological:

3. Slang:

4. Science:

5. How do the definitions differ?

Locating Print and Electronic Encyclopedias

3-6

An encyclopedia contains articles written by experts on a variety of subjects. The articles are arranged in alphabetical order by topic. There are five basic types of encyclopedias. Knowing how each is different will help you decide when to use each.

General encyclopedias include overview articles on a wide range of topics. The articles are arranged alphabetically in a set of volumes. Illustrations are also included. The last volume in the set is the index. Information is kept up to date with yearbooks or supplements. An example of a general encyclopedia is the *Encyclopedia Americana*.

Single-volume encyclopedias include short articles arranged in alphabetical order. There is no index or table of contents. An example of a single-volume encyclopedia is the *Random House Encyclopedia*.

Encyclopedias for children and young adults are general encyclopedias that are written and designed for a specific age group. There are many illustrations and study aids and they are easier to read than other encyclopedias. An example of an encyclopedia for children and young adults is the *World Book Encyclopedia*.

Foreign-language encyclopedias are found in three forms:

1. Encyclopedias written from the perspective of another country and published in the language of that country, such as *Enzyklopadie Brockhaus*.

2. Encyclopedias written from the perspective of another country but translated into English, such as the *Great Soviet Encyclopedia*.

3. Encyclopedias published in the United States but in a foreign language, such as the *Chinese Language Concise Encyclopaedia Britannica*.

Subject encyclopedias are found for many subjects, such as medicine, psychology, art, music, business, science, and technology. The articles are longer, more complete, and more technical than those found in general encyclopedias. An example of a subject encyclopedia is the *McGraw-Hill Encyclopedia of Science and Technology*.

3-6 *Locating Print and Electronic Encyclopedias (continued)*

Now find another example of each of type of encyclopedia. Write its title and call number. Include a location with the call number if provided. Then ✔ Print or Electronic to show the format of the encyclopedia.

General Encyclopedia

Title

Call number   Print _____   Electronic _____

Single-Volume Encyclopedia

Title

Call number   Print _____   Electronic _____

Encyclopedia for Children and Young Adults

Title

Call number   Print _____   Electronic _____

Foreign-Language Encyclopedia

Title

Call number   Print _____   Electronic _____

Subject Encyclopedia

Title

Call number   Print _____   Electronic _____

Using a Print Encyclopedia

3-7

When you look for information in a print encyclopedia, begin by selecting the most important word in your topic. This word is your **keyword**. Look for your keyword in the index to the encyclopedia. The index is usually the last volume. Select another keyword if you cannot find your first keyword in the index.

For example, using the keyword *rap* from the topic "rap music in America," you might find the following index entry. Study this sample index entry and answer the questions.

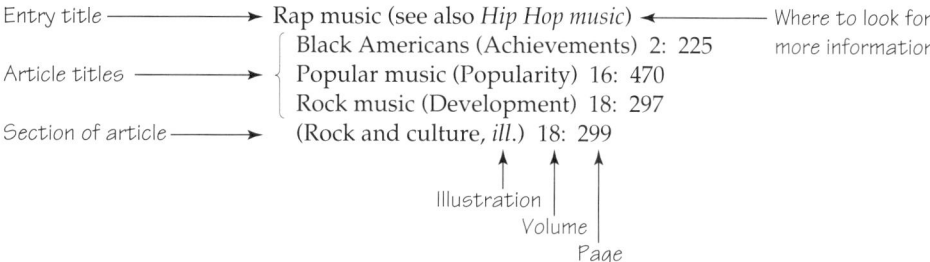

1. In what articles will you find information about the topic?

2. In the article "Black Americans," under what section will you find information about the topic?

3. In what volume number and on what page will you find the information about the popularity of rap music?

4. In what volume and on what page will you find an illustration relating to rap music?

5. Where would you look for more information about the topic?

Comparing Information from Print Encyclopedias   3-8

Look up the topic "endangered animals" in both a general encyclopedia and a subject encyclopedia. Then answer the following.

1. What are the titles of the encyclopedias used?

   General: Subject:

2. What keyword(s) did you use?

   General: Subject:

3. What are the titles and sections of the articles with information on the topic?

   General: Subject:

4. What kind of pictures did you find on the topic?

   General: Subject:

5. Describe any other graphic aids that you found that complement the text.

   General: Subject:

6. Did you find a bibliography or reading list for the topic?

   General: Subject:

7. What did you learn about general and subject encyclopedias?

Using a Multimedia Encyclopedia

3-9

A **multimedia encyclopedia** provides information in addition to the text. Here are some examples of the different types of media information found by using a multimedia encyclopedia. Next to each is an **icon** for that function. An icon is a hyper linked picture used in a computer database that stands for a specific function. For example, the icon means that you can click on it to hear sound. Here are examples of other icons used in multimedia. Next to each icon is an example of information you might find when you click on the icon.

Icon	Information	
📹	video	**Example**: Scenes of hurricanes and the destruction they cause.
🔊	sound	**Examples**: Alligator growl; orchestra playing a Beethoven symphony; audio broadcast of astronaut during first moon landing.
🎞	animation	**Example**: Diagram of how a rocket works showing various stages and narrated with an explanation of each step in the process.
🖼	picture	**Example**: Photograph of a platypus, or of the skyline of Munich, or of Richard Nixon.
🌐	map	**Example**: Map of the Middle East with names of places hyperlinked.
📊	table/chart/graph	**Examples**: Chart showing endangered plants and animals; graph showing world population; table showing characteristics of the moon.

A multimedia encyclopedia is searched by keyword(s) or by browsing categories. You may also use Boolean connectors to narrow your search. For example, *art* and *Africa* might find information about sculptures from Nigeria, art festivals in Tunisia, or jewelry from Benin.

Other features provided by multimedia encyclopedias include an outline of the article; a timeline of events; and related articles.

3-9 *Using a Multimedia Encyclopedia (continued)*

Use a multimedia encyclopedia to look up the country Haiti. Complete the following:

1. Did you find a map of the country?

2. Did you find a picture of the flag?

3. Did you find an outline for the article?

4. Did you find information about Haiti in related articles?

5. Describe the photographs you found.

6. Was any information arranged in charts or tables or graphs?

7. Describe any sounds or videos you found about Haiti.

8. What other interesting features did you use in the multimedia encyclopedia to find information about Haiti?

Comparing Information from Print and Multimedia Encyclopedias   3-10

Look up the topic "rap music in America" in both a general print encyclopedia and a multimedia encyclopedia. Complete the following.

1. What are the titles of the two encyclopedias used?

   Print encyclopedia:

   Multimedia encyclopedia:

2. What differences were there in the type and amount of information you found in the two encyclopedias?

3. Which encyclopedia was more useful in learning about the topic? Why?

Locating Almanacs 3-11

An **almanac** is a single-volume reference book containing facts, data, tables, charts, lists, and other methods of organizing useful information. Almanacs provide information about a wide range of topics. Some of the most frequently used almanacs are:

> *Information Please Almanac*
> *New York Public Library Desk Reference*
> *Universal Almanac*
> *Whitaker's Almanack*
> *World Almanac and Book of Facts*

Look up the current volume for each of these almanacs in your library. For each, write its title and call number. Include a location with the call number if provided.

1. Title:

    Call number:

2. Title:

    Call number:

3. Title:

    Call number:

4. Title:

    Call number:

5. Title:

    Call number:

Some almanacs are for specific subjects—for example, the *African American Almanac*. Use your library catalog to identify a subject almanac in your library.

6. Title:

    Call number:

Using Almanacs

3-12

Use an almanac to answer the questions that follow. You may need to look in more than one almanac to find the answer. For each question, write the answer to the question and the title of the almanac containing the information needed to answer the question. Also include the page number(s) where the information appears in the almanac.

1. What is the highest mountain in Europe? How tall is it?

2. How many votes were cast for Bill Clinton in Big Horn, Montana, in the 1996 presidential election?

3. What is the highest temperature ever recorded in the state of California?

4. What was the top-selling passenger car in the United States in 1995?

5. Who invented the electric razor? In what year?

6. What baseball team won the World Series in 1947? What team did they defeat?

7. What have you learned about almanacs?

Locating Statistical Sources 3-13

A **statistical source** contains statistics on different topics. The statistics are presented in tables, charts, and graphs. The statistics are abstracted from longer reports. The reference for the longer report is provided on the page with the table, chart, or graph. Some statistical sources are general, and others are specialized.

General statistical sources include statistics on many topics. Two frequently used statistical sources are:

> *Statistical Abstract of the United States*
> *Statistical Yearbook* (United Nations)

Look up the current volume for *Statistical Abstract of the United States* in your library. Write its title and call number. Include a location with the call number if provided.

1. Title:

    Call number:

Statistical abstracts for the individual states are also general statistical sources. Look up the statistical abstract for your state. Write its title and call number. Include a location with the call number if provided.

2. Title:

    Call number:

Specialized statistical sources include statistics on a specific topic. An example is the *Digest of Education Statistics*. Use your library catalog to identify a specialized statistics source. Write its title and call number.

3. Title:

    Call number:

Using Statistical Abstract of the United States

3-14

Statistical Abstract of the United States is the most important source of statistics for the United States. The statistics are collected and compiled by the U.S. government and are reliable. The statistics are presented in tables, charts, and graphs. The source is always provided with the table, chart, or graph.

Using the most current volume of the *Statistical Abstract of the United States*, follow these steps to answer the questions.

Steps

1. Use the index in the back of the book to look up your topic. Be creative with your keywords.
2. Go to the table numbers provided. The number given is the table number, not the page number.
3. Look at all the tables listed in the index on your topic to find the right one to answer your question.
4. Refer to 4–1 through 4–4 if you do not know how to read a table.

Questions

1. How many total new cases of lung cancer were there in 1996?

    Answer:

    Table number: Page number:

    Source:

2. What was the average sale price of a one-family home in Tucson, Arizona, in 1994?

    Answer:

    Table number: Page number:

    Source:

3. How many high school dropouts were there in 1994?

    Answer:

    Table number: Page number:

    Source:

Locating Print and Electronic Atlases   3-15

An **atlas** is a collection of maps. There are four basic types of atlases. Each has its own value. Knowing about the different types will help you decide when to use each. Some atlases are available in electronic format.

General World Atlas. General world atlases contain maps showing physical and political features of countries throughout the world. Most general world atlases include sections of maps on specific topics such as climate, population, and health. An example of a general atlas is the *Hammond Atlas of the World*.

Historical Atlas. Historical atlases contain maps that portray an event or show how something developed or changed over a period of time. Historical atlases include information about topics such as changes in borders, military campaigns, exploration, and culture. An historical atlas usually has the word *history* or *historical* in its title. An example of a historical atlas is the *Times Atlas of World History*.

Subject Atlas. Subject atlases contain maps related to a specific place, such as the *National Atlas of Canada*, or about a topic, such as the *Atlas of the Christian Church*.

Road Atlas. Road atlases contain maps that show major highways and secondary roads for a geographical area. An example of a road atlas is the *Rand McNally Road Atlas*.

Find another example of each of type of atlas. Write its title and call number. Include a location with the call number if provided. Then ✔ Print or Electronic to show the format.

General Atlas

Title:

Call number: Print _____   Electronic _____

Historical Atlas

Title:

Call number: Print _____   Electronic _____

Subject Atlas

Title:

Call number: Print _____   Electronic _____

Road Atlas

Title:

Call number: Print _____   Electronic _____

Using Print Atlases

Use an atlas to answer the questions that follow. You may need to look in more than one atlas to find the answer. For each question, write the answer to the question and the title of the atlas in which you found the answer. Also include the page number(s) where the information appears in the atlas.

1. What are the names of the countries that border Yemen?

    Answer:

    Title of atlas:

    Page(s):

2. What is the name of the river that flows through the Nubian Desert?

    Answer:

    Title of atlas:

    Page(s):

3. Find a map that shows the population of a place. It can be a city, state, or country. What is the name of this place and its population?

    Answer:

    Title of atlas:

    Page(s):

4. What is the name of the desert on the China–Mongolia border?

    Answer:

    Title of atlas:

    Page(s):

Using Electronic Atlases 3-17

Atlases in electronic formats can be found on CD ROM and on the Internet. Some electronic atlases are multimedia.

Some popular atlases on CD ROM are:

> Encarta 97 World Atlas
> 3D Atlas
> National Geographic Picture Atlas of the World

A popular atlas on the WWW is *Map Machine Atlas* from the National Geographic Society. It can be found at:

> http://www.nationalgeographic.com/resources/ngo/maps/atlas/index.html

Use an electronic atlas to look up the country Sudan. Then answer the questions about the information you find in the atlas about Sudan.

1. Did you find a political map of the country?

2. Did you find a physical map of the country?

3. Describe any other maps you found for Sudan:

4. Can you find the map by typing in the name?

5. Can you *zoom in* by clicking on the area of a larger map?

6. Did you find an article about Sudan?

7. Describe any photographs you found:

8. Was any information arranged in charts or tables or graphs?

9. What other interesting feature did you use in the electronic atlas to find information about Sudan?

Locating Biographical Sources   3-18

Biographical sources are reference books that provide information about the lives and accomplishments of famous people, living or dead. Some biographical sources are general and others are specialized. Some biographical sources are available in electronic format.

General biographical sources include biographical information for all types of famous people from all fields. Here are some common general biographical sources.

    Dictionary of International Biography   *Grolier Library of North American Biographies*
    Current Biography   *Cambridge Dictionary of American Biography*
    Webster's Biographical Dictionary   *McGraw-Hill Encyclopedia of World Biography*

Find three of these biographical sources in your library. Write each title and call number. Include a location with the call number if provided.

    1. Title:

       Call number:

    2. Title:

       Call number:

    3. Title:

       Call number:

Specialized biographical sources include biographical information for a specific population, such as women, or a specific field, such as artists. An example of a specialized biographical source is the *Dictionary of Scientific Biography*. Use your library catalog to identify another specialized biographical source.

    4. Title:

       Call number:

Electronic biographical sources are available on CD ROM or on the Internet. One common biographical source on CD ROM is U X L Biographies®.

    5. Check to see if your library owns another biographical source in electronic format. If it does, write the title here.

Copyright © 1999 by Allyn and Bacon.

Using Biographical Sources   3-19

Use **biographical sources** to find information about these famous people. Next to each person's name, write the title of the biographical source containing information about that person. Also write the page number(s) where the information appears. If there is a volume number or date, write that too.

	Title of Biographical Source	*Volume/Date/Page(s)*
Harriet Tubman		
Jackie Robinson		
Cesar Chavez		
John Glenn		
Vasco da Gama		
Louisa May Alcott		
Dorothea Dix		
Desmond Mpilo Tutu		
Elizabeth Blackwell		
Sandra Day O'Connor		
Jim Thorpe		
Frederick Douglass		

Locating Chronologies   3-20

A **chronology** presents information organized by date. Chronologies may cover events over a long period of time, such as hundreds of years, or as short a period as one year. Most chronologies present the information in tables. Some chronologies are general and others are specialized.

General chronologies include information on many topics and over a long period of time. Here are some common chronologies:

> *People's Chronology*
> *Timetables of History: A Horizontal Linkage of People and Events*
> *New York Public Library Book of Chronologies*
> *Chronology of the Modern World, 1763–1992*
> *Asimov's Chronology of the World*
> *Historical Tables, 58 B.C.–A.D. 1985*

Look up three of these chronologies in your library. Write down each title and call number. Include a location with the call number if provided.

1. Title:

    Call number:

2. Title:

    Call number:

3. Title:

    Call number:

Specialized chronologies include information on specific subjects or over short periods of time. Examples of specialized chronologies are:

> *Timetables of Technology*
> *Day by Day: The Sixties*

Use your library catalog to identify another specialized chronology.

4. Title:

    Call number:

Using Chronologies   3-21

Use a chronology to answer the questions that follow. You may need to look in more than one chronology to find the answer. For each question, write the answer to the question and the title of the chronology used to answer the question.

1. Describe an important event in science or technology that happened in 1839.

    Answer:

    Title of chronology:

2. Describe something important that happened in race relations in the United States in 1967.

    Answer:

    Title of chronology:

3. What was a major event about food in 1756?

    Answer:

    Title of chronology:

4. Describe a significant event in world history in 1212.

    Answer:

    Title of chronology:

Locating Reference Sources for Literary Criticism   3-22

Reference sources for literary criticism provide summarized criticism of an author's work. Some reference sources for literary criticism are general and others are specialized. Biographical reference sources for literary criticism provide biographical information in addition to literary criticism. Some reference sources for literary criticism are available in electronic format.

General reference sources for literary criticism include information for all categories of literature, such as plays, poetry, short stories, and novels. Here are some common reference sources for literary criticism.

Contemporary Literary Criticism   *World Literature Criticism*
Twentieth-Century Literary Criticism   *Nineteenth-Century Literary Criticism*

Find two of these reference sources for literary criticism in your library. Write each title and call number. Include a location with the call number if provided.

1. Title:

    Call number:

2. Title:

    Call number:

Specialized reference sources for literary criticism include information for one category of literature only. An example of a specialized reference source for literary criticism is *Short Story Criticism*. Use your library catalog to identify another specialized reference source for literary criticism.

3. Title:

    Call number:

Biographical reference sources for literary criticism include biographical information about writers and a list of their works in addition to literary criticism. An example of a biographical source for literary criticism is *Dictionary of Literary Biography*. Use your library catalog to identify a biographical source for literary criticism.

4. Title:

    Call number:

Electronic reference sources for literary criticism are available on CD ROM and on the Internet. One common source on CD ROM is *DISCovering Authors*®. This source is also available for younger readers as *Junior DISCovering Authors*®.

5. Write down the title of an electronic reference source for literary criticism that your library owns.

Using Reference Sources for Literary Criticism

3-23

Use a reference source for literary criticism to find criticism of the works of one of the following authors. Read the criticism and summarize three major themes in the author's works. You may need to look in more than one source to find criticism about the author you selected.

    Mary Wollstonecraft Shelley   Zora Neale Hurston   Ernest Hemingway
    Robert Frost   Amy Tan   Pablo Neruda

Author selected:

Theme 1:

Theme 2:

Theme 3:

Using Reference Sources

3-24

Write the type of reference source you could use to find each of the following. For example, a dictionary of slang could be used to look up the definition of *dis*.

1. An extensive definition of Boolean logic:

2. Important events in music between 1700 and 1900:

3. Amount of trade in dollars between the United States and Costa Rica:

4. The boundaries of eastern European countries:

5. An overview of the life and works of Ernest Hemingway:

6. The definition of the word *epistemology*:

7. An overview article about the Louisiana Purchase:

8. A map that shows the battles of the Civil War:

9. A short article about the Internet:

10. The birth and death dates of Mahatma Gandhi:

11. A list of the five longest rivers in the world:

12. Critical evaluation of Shakespeare's plays:

13. An overview article about World War II written in German:

14. Statistics about average income for women and men:

15. A long, detailed article about Expressionism in art:

Copyright © 1999 by Allyn and Bacon.

Answer Key

3-1 1. Subject dictionary. 2. General encyclopedias include overview articles on a wide range of topics, and subject encyclopedias are for specific subjects and include articles that are longer, more complete, and more technical than those found in general encyclopedias. 3. Almanac or statistical source. 4. Unabridged dictionary. 5. Chronology. 6. Atlas. 7. Shortened forms of unabridged dictionaries in which infrequently used words are omitted. 8. When you need concise background information about the lives and accomplishments of famous people, living or dead, and you do not need or cannot find an entire book about them. 9. Sources for literary criticism. 10. To find a map that portrays an event or shows how something has developed or changed over a period of time. 11. General encyclopedia. 12. Encyclopedias in a foreign language or about a foreign country. 13. Maps related to a specific place or about a topic.

3-2 Answers will vary.

3-3 Answers will vary.

3-4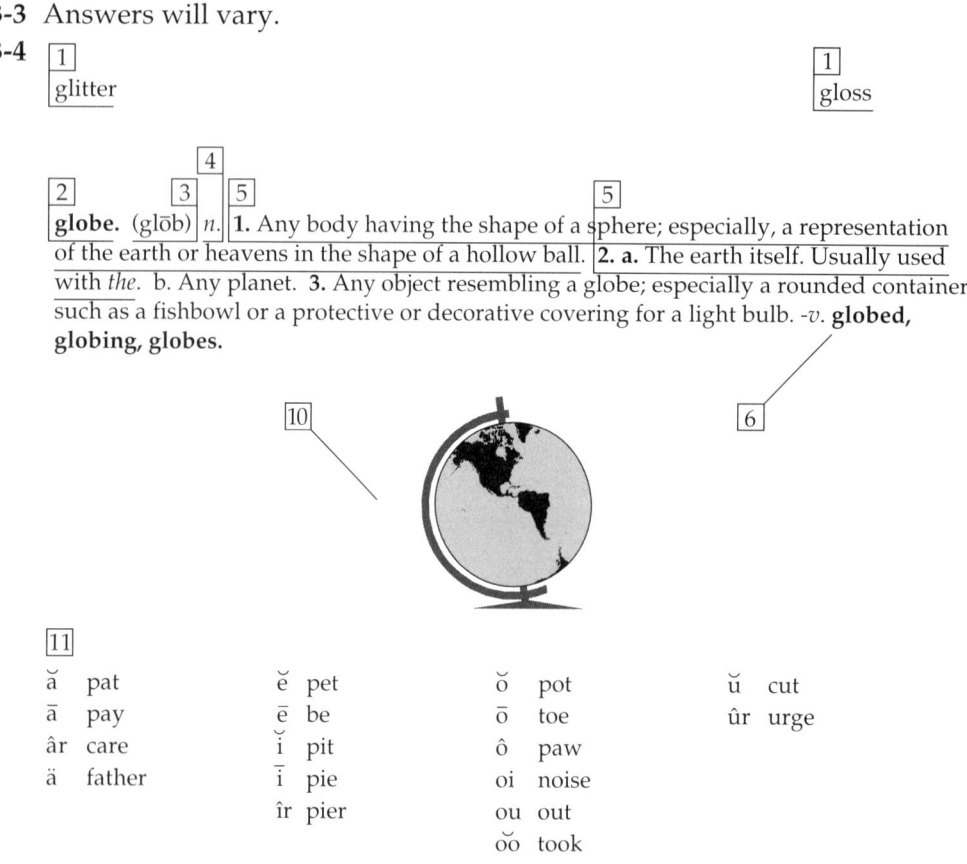

3-5 Answers will vary with the dictionary used, but the summary might include definitions of *radical* such as the following:

abridged: Arising from or going to a root or source.

etymological: The fourteenth-century meaning is the moisture or natural essence of plants and animals that contribute to their vitality.

slang: Originally from surfers' slang, at or exceeding the limits of safety, such as "far out"

science (in chemistry): A group of atoms in a compound or alone; (in mathematics): A root of a number.

3-6 Answers will vary.

3-7 1. Black Americans; Popular music; Rock music. 2. Achievements. 3. Volume 16, page 470. 4. Volume 18, page 299. 5. Hip Hop music.
3-8 Answers will vary.
3-9 Answers will vary.
3-10 Answers will vary.
3-11 Answers will vary.
3-12 Answers might vary slightly with almanac used, but sample answers for 1 through 6 are: 1. Mont Blanc, France/Italy, 15,771 feet 2. 2,453. 3. 106 degrees. 4. Ford Taurus. 5. Schick, 1917. 6. The New York Yankees beat the Brooklyn Dodgers. 7. Answers will vary.
3-13 Answers will vary.
3-14 Table numbers and pages will vary with edition used, but answers and sources are as follows: 1. 177,000. The source is U.S. National Institutes of Health, National Cancer Institute, Cancer Statistics Review, Annual. 2. $152,800. The source is U.S. Bureau of the Census, Current Construction Reports, series C21. 3. 3,820,000. The source is U.S. Bureau of the Census, Current Population Reports, P20-487 and earlier reports.
3-15 Answers will vary.
3-16 1. Oman and Saudi Arabia; atlases and page numbers will vary. 2. Nile; atlases and page numbers will vary. 3. Answers will vary. 4. Gobi Desert; atlases and page numbers will vary.
3-17 Answers will vary.
3-18 Answers will vary.
3-19 Answers will vary with biographical sources used. Sample answers are:
Harriet Tubman—*McGraw-Hill Encyclopedia of World Biography*, Vol. 2, p. 13.
Jackie Robinson—*Cambridge Dictionary of American Biography*, 1995, p. 618.
Cesar Chavez—*Cambridge Dictionary of American Biography*, 1995, p. 129.
John Glenn—*Cambridge Dictionary of American Biography*, 1995, p. 276.
Vasco da Gama—*Webster's Biographical Dictionary*, 1970, p. 573.
Louisa May Alcott—*McGraw-Hill Encyclopedia of World Biography*, Vol. 1, p. 100.
Dorothea Dix—*McGraw-Hill Encyclopedia of World Biography*, Vol. 3, p. 394.
Desmond Mpilo Tutu—*Current Biography*, 1981–85, p. 418.
Elizabeth Blackwell—*McGraw-Hill Encyclopedia of World Biography*, Vol. 2, p. 7.
Sandra Day O'Connor—*Current Biography*, 1982, p. 297.
Jim Thorpe—*Current Biography*, 1950, p. 569.
Frederick Douglass—*Cambridge Dictionary of American Biography*, Vol. 3, p. 406.
3-20 Answers will vary.
3-21 Answers will vary with chronology used and events selected. Sample answers are: 1. The metallic element lanthanum was discovered by Carl Gustav Mosander; from the *Timetables of History*. 2. Race riots broke out in 127 U.S. cities, killing at least 77 people and injuring almost 4,000; from the *People's Chronology*. 3. The first chocolate factory opened (in Germany); from *Historical Tables*, 58 B.C.–A.D. 1985. 4. Kings of Castile, Aragon, and Navarre defeated the Moors, from *Historical Tables, 58* B.C.–A.D., 1985.
3-22 Answers will vary.
3-23 Themes will vary.
3-24 Best answers are: 1. Subject dictionary. 2. Chronology. 3. Almanac, statistical source 4. Atlas. 5. Biographical source. 6. Etymological dictionary. 7. General encyclopedia. 8. Historical atlas. 9. Single-volume encyclopedia. 10. Biographical source. 11. Almanac. 12. Reference source for literary criticism. 13. Foreign-language encyclopedia. 14. Statistical source. 15. Subject encyclopedia.

CHAPTER FOUR

Interpreting Visual Information from Reference Sources

CHAPTER OBJECTIVES

1. Teach students the different ways that information can be presented visually.
2. Teach students to interpret information presented visually in reference sources.

TITLES OF REPRODUCIBLE ACTIVITIES

4-1 Tables
4-2 Another Table
4-3 A Complex Table
4-4 Bar Graphs
4-5 Line Graphs
4-6 Pie Graphs
4-7 Organizational Charts
4-8 Time Lines
4-9 Diagrams
4-10 Political and Physical Maps
4-11 Data Maps
    Answer Key

USING THE REPRODUCIBLE ACTIVITIES

Use activities 4-1 through 4-3 to teach students how to interpret information presented in tables. Each activity introduces a table with a different numerical unit. Use 4-4 through 4-6 to teach students to interpret information presented in different types of graphs. Use activity 4-7 to teach students how to interpret an organizational chart and activity 4-8 to introduce time lines. Use activity 4-9 to teach students to interpret information from diagrams and 4-10 and 4-11 to interpret political, physical, and data maps.

4-1 Tables

Tell students that tables are used to present data. Explain that reference sources they learned about in Chapter Three, such as the *Statistical Abstract of the United States* and various almanacs, use many tables to present data. Have students read the introductory information about tables. The table presented is part of a table published in the *Statistical Abstract of the United States*. The table lists three categories of cheese: American, Italian, and Other. Tell students to pay attention to the footnote below the table. Also point out the source of the information below the table, and tell students that the source is important to consider as they evaluate the information as well as when they need to find more information on the topic. Then point out the different parts of the table. Explain how to interpret the data found in this table. Then have students complete the activity.

4-2 Another Table

Use this activity to provide students with additional practice interpreting information found in a table. Explain how to interpret the data found in this table. Then have students complete the activity.

4-3 A Complex Table

Because of the complexity of this table, this activity works best when it follows 4-1 and 4-2.

Explain to students that some tables can be very complex because they contain many categories of data shown in multiple columns. Explain to students that tables from statistical reference sources are particularly complex. Explain how to interpret the data found in this table. Then have students complete the activity.

You may extend this activity by also using activity 3-14 in which students learn about the *Statistical Abstract of the United States*. You may also extend this activity by providing an additional question for students to answer using the *Statistical Abstract of the United States*.

4-4 Bar Graphs

Tell students that bar graphs are used to show the relationships between sets of facts. Show students the different parts of a bar graph. Point out that some bar graphs are presented horizontally. Explain how interpretations are made using data from bar graphs. Then have students use the bar graph to answer the questions.

4-5 Line Graphs

Explain that line graphs are used to show trends over a period of time. Show students the different parts of a line graph. Explain how interpretations are made using data from line graphs. Then have students use the line graph to answer the questions.

4-6 Pie Graphs

Tell students the term *pie graph* is used because this type of graph looks like a pie divided into slices. Explain that the parts must add up to 100 percent. Also explain why some pie graphs have a part labeled "Other." Explain how interpretations are made using data from pie graphs. Then have students use the pie graph to answer the questions.

4-7 Organizational Charts

Tell students that organizational charts show how positions within an organization are related to each other. Explain how boxes and lines are use to present the information and to show reporting relationships. Tell students that they will find organizational charts for businesses, government, and other organizations. Then have students use the organizational chart to answer the questions.

4-8 Time Lines

Tell students that a time line shows the relationship between events over time and shows when important events took place. Point out that most time lines are shown from left to right, but some are displayed from top to bottom. Explain how interpretations are made using data from time lines. Have students use the time line to answer the questions.

4-9 Diagrams

Tell students that diagrams are used to show the parts of something. Explain that sometimes the parts are labeled and sometimes the parts are identified in a key. Explain how interpretations are made using data from diagrams. Tell students about reference sources that have many diagrams to explain how things work. Then have students answer the questions.

4-10 Political and Physical Maps

Explain that political maps show the political divisions within a country such as boundaries. Explain that physical maps show the features of the earth's surface such as mountains, highlands, plateaus, rivers, and major bodies of water. Point out that the date of a political map is especially important because of changes in borders, creation of new countries, and name changes. Have students use the political and physical maps of South America to answer the questions.

4-11 Data Maps

Explain that maps are often used to present facts or data visually. Tell students that many topical or subject atlases they learned about in Chapter Three include data maps. Explain how interpretations are made using data maps. Have students answer the questions.

Tables

4-1

Tables are used to show facts or data that would be difficult to understand if they were presented in written form. A table has a title that explains its purpose. Information at the top of the table clarifies the numeric unit used in the table (e.g., in pounds, in percent, in thousands). The data is presented in columns. Each column has a heading. Sometimes, footnotes are listed below the table. The source of the data is also found below the table. Use the table to answer the questions.

U.S. Per Capita Consumption of Major Food Commodities: 1970 to 1994

In pounds, retail weight

Commodity	1970	1975	1980	1985	1990	1992	1993	1994
Cheese	11.4	14.3	17.5	22.5	24.6	26.0	26.3	26.8
American	7.0	8.2	9.6	12.2	11.1	11.3	11.4	11.6
Cheddar	5.8	6.0	6.9	9.8	9.0	9.2	9.1	9.1
Italian	2.1	3.2	4.4	6.5	9.0	10.0	9.8	10.3
Mozzarella	1.2	2.1	3.0	4.6	6.9	7.7	7.6	7.9
Other	2.3	2.9	3.4	3.9	4.5	4.7	5.0	5.0
Swiss	0.9	1.1	1.3	1.3	1.4	1.2	1.2	1.2
Cream and Neufchatel	0.6	0.7	1.0	1.2	1.7	2.0	2.1	2.2

Note: Excludes cottage, pot, and baker's cheese. Includes other cheeses not shown separately.
Source: U.S. Department of Agriculture. Economic Research Service. *Food Consumption, Prices, and Expenditures, 1996: Annual Data, 1970–1994.* Statistical Bulletin No. 928, April 1, 1996.

1. Was more American cheese or Italian cheese consumed in 1994?

2. How much mozzarella was consumed per person in the United States in 1970? In 1994?

3. Does this data include information about how much cottage cheese was consumed?

4. What kinds of cheese are people eating less in 1994 than in 1985?

5. Write the name of the source where you can probably find data for 1972.

Copyright © 1999 by Allyn and Bacon.

Another Table 4-2

Some tables present data in percentages. The table has a title, an explanation of the numeric unit, and data presented in columns. The source of the data is cited at the bottom of the table. Use the table to answer the questions.

Home Ownership Rates, by State, 1984 to 1995 (in percent)

State	1984	1990	1995	State	1984	1990	1995
United States	64.5	64.1	64.7	Missouri	69.5	64.2	69.4
Alabama	73.7	69.9	70.1	Montana	66.4	69.6	68.7
Alaska	57.6	57.1	60.9	Nebraska	69.3	67.5	67.1
Arizona	65.2	66.3	62.9	Nevada	58.9	55.8	58.6
Arkansas	65.9	68.6	67.2	New Hampshire	67.1	66.8	66.0
California	53.7	54.5	55.4	New Jersey	63.4	64.8	64.9
Colorado	64.7	59.8	64.6	New Mexico	68.0	69.5	67.0
Connecticut	67.8	65.5	68.2	New York	51.1	52.6	52.7
Delaware	70.4	70.2	71.7	North Carolina	68.8	69.3	70.1
District of Columbia	37.3	35.1	38.2	North Dakota	70.1	65.4	67.3
Florida	66.5	66.1	66.6	Ohio	67.7	68.7	67.9
Georgia	63.6	65.7	66.6	Oklahoma	71.0	69.2	69.8
Hawaii	50.7	55.2	50.2	Oregon	61.9	65.2	63.2
Idaho	69.7	68.4	72.0	Pennsylvania	71.1	74.0	71.5
Illinois	62.4	63.0	66.4	Rhode Island	60.9	58.2	57.9
Indiana	69.9	66.1	71.0	South Carolina	69.1	73.1	71.3
Iowa	71.3	68.4	71.4	South Dakota	69.6	66.1	67.5
Kansas	72.7	69.7	67.5	Tennessee	67.6	68.0	67.0
Kentucky	70.2	67.2	71.2	Texas	62.5	59.0	61.4
Louisiana	70.1	68.9	65.3	Utah	69.9	70.7	71.5
Maine	74.1	72.0	76.7	Vermont	66.9	70.8	70.4
Maryland	67.8	63.8	65.8	Virginia	68.3	68.9	68.1
Massachusetts	61.7	60.2	60.2	Washington	65.7	61.8	61.6
Michigan	72.7	70.6	72.2	West Virginia	72.0	72.4	73.1
Minnesota	72.6	68.9	73.3	Wisconsin	65.2	68.9	67.5
Mississippi	72.3	71.8	71.1	Wyoming	68.8	68.7	69.0

Source: U.S. Bureau of the Census, *Current Housing Report*, Series H111/95-A.

1. What state had the highest percentage of homeowners in 1995?

2. Excluding the District of Columbia, what state had the lowest percentage of homeowners in 1995?

3. What percentage of the population in the District of Columbia were not homeowners in 1995?

4. By how many percentage points did home ownership increase in Connecticut from 1984 to 1995?

5. What is the source for the data in this table?

A Complex Table

Some tables contain many categories of data shown in multiple columns. Use the table to answer the questions.

College Enrollment, by Sex and Attendance Status, 1983–1993 (as of Fall, in Thousands)

Sex and Age	1983 Total	1983 Part time	1988 Total	1988 Part time	1989 Total	1989 Part time	1991 Total	1991 Part time	1993, Preliminary Total	1993, Preliminary Part time
Total	12,465	5,204	13,055	5,619	13,539	5,878	14,359	6,244	14,305	6,178
Male	6,024	2,264	6,002	2,340	6,190	2,450	6,502	2,573	6,427	2,537
14 to 17 years old	102	16	55	5	71	12	46	6	83	10
18 to 19 years old	1,256	158	1,290	132	1,342	113	1,217	121	1,224	138
20 to 21 years old	1,241	205	1,243	216	1,189	198	1,306	230	1,294	209
22 to 24 years old	1,158	382	1,106	378	1,090	367	1,214	378	1,260	392
25 to 29 years old	1,115	624	875	485	1,038	639	1,082	587	950	564
30 to 34 years old	570	384	617	456	603	439	664	475	661	484
35 years and over	583	494	816	668	857	682	972	775	955	739
Female	6,441	2,940	7,053	3,278	7,349	3,428	7,857	3,672	7,877	3,641
14 to 17 years old	142	16	115	17	101	12	76	1	93	6
18 to 19 years old	1,496	179	1,536	195	1,515	184	1,496	185	1,416	172
20 to 21 years old	1,125	204	1,278	218	1,253	213	1,462	239	1,414	279
22 to 24 years old	884	378	932	403	1,104	470	1,072	412	1,263	493
25 to 29 years old	947	658	932	633	1,052	732	1,053	679	1,058	689
30 to 34 years old	721	553	698	499	750	563	804	593	811	575
35 years old and over	1,126	953	1,563	1,313	1,574	1,253	1,895	1,564	1,824	1,427

Source: U.S. National Center for Education Statistics. *Digest of Education Statistics*, annual.

1. In total, were there more males or females enrolled in college in the fall of 1993?

2. In total, how many females aged 35 and over were enrolled in college in the fall of 1993? Males 35 and over?

3. How many more part-time students were enrolled in the fall of 1993 than in 1983?

4. For 1991, what percentage of total students enrolled were part-time students?

5. What is the source for the data in this table?

Bar Graphs   4-4

Bar graphs use bars to show the relationships between sets of facts. A bar graph has a title at the top and labels on the left-hand side and bottom. On the bottom of the graph there is a number line. The length of each bar shows how much the bar stands for. Use the bar graph to answer the questions.

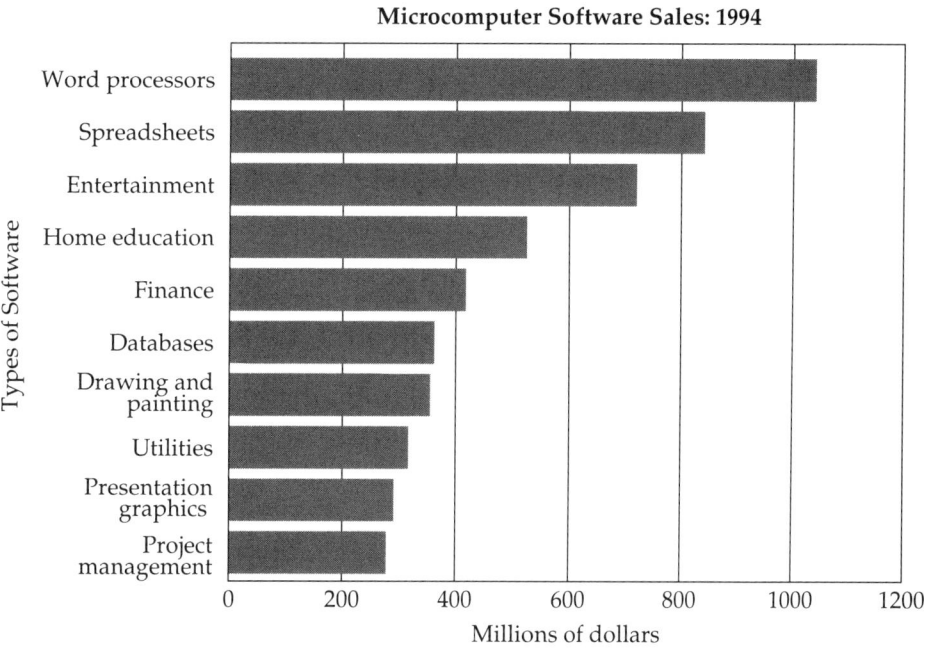

Source: U.S. government.

1. What is this bar graph about?

2. What do the bars stand for?

3. What do the numbers stand for?

4. Which type of software sold the most in 1994?

5. For which type of software were sales about $400 million?

6. Which sold more, entertainment or database software?

7. What were the combined sales for home education and finance software?

Line Graphs

4-5

Line graphs are used to show trends over a period of time. Read the title of the graph shown to learn what it is about. Then look to learn what information is presented on the left side and along the bottom. The lines on the graph show trends in federal government outlays (spending) and receipts (income). The different between outlays and receipts represents the federal deficit (more spending than income). Use the line graph to answer the questions.

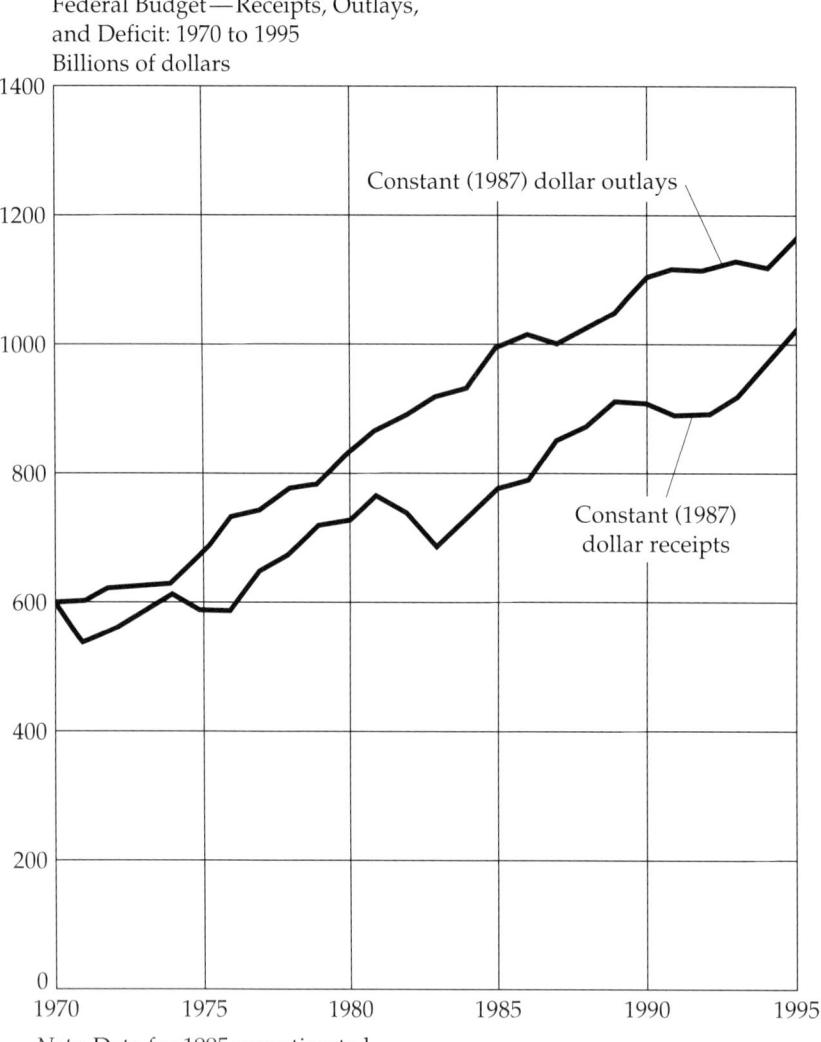

1. What three types of information are shown in the line graph?
2. What has been the trend in federal government spending?
3. What has been the trend in federal government income?
4. What has happened to the federal deficit since 1970?
5. What happened to federal income in approximately 1981–1982?
6. What was the approximate size of the deficit in 1995?

Pie Graphs

4-6

Pie graphs look like a pie divided into slices. The title tells the subject of the pie graph. Each part of a pie graph shows how much of the whole it stands for. The parts must equal the whole and must add up to 100 percent. Very small parts are often combined and called "Others." This is done because it is difficult to show a very small part of something.

Examine this pie graph and answer the questions.

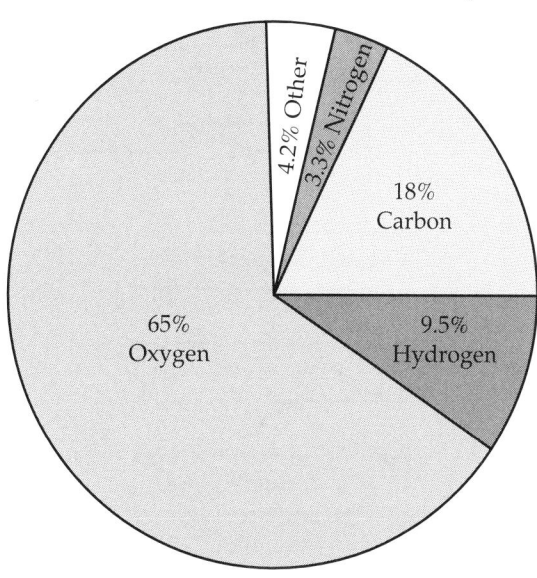

1. What does this pie graph show?

2. Which chemical is found in the greatest amount in the human body?

3. Is there a higher amount of hydrogen or carbon in the human body?

4. Oxygen plus carbon make up what percentage of the chemical elements in the human body?

5. About one-fifth of the chemical elements in the body consist of which element?

6. Oxygen and hydrogen combine to form water in the human body. About what percentage of the human body is water?

7. The parts shown in a pie graph must add up to what percentage?

8. Why is there a category called "Other"?

Copyright © 1999 by Allyn and Bacon.

Organizational Charts   4-7

Organizational charts are used to show how things are organized. Information is presented in boxes. Each box is labeled to show what it presents. Lines are used to show how the boxes are related.

Look at the following organizational chart. It shows how the U.S. government is organized to do its work. The boxes contain facts about the government. The lines show how the facts go together. By studying the chart you see how the government works. Use the chart to answer the questions.

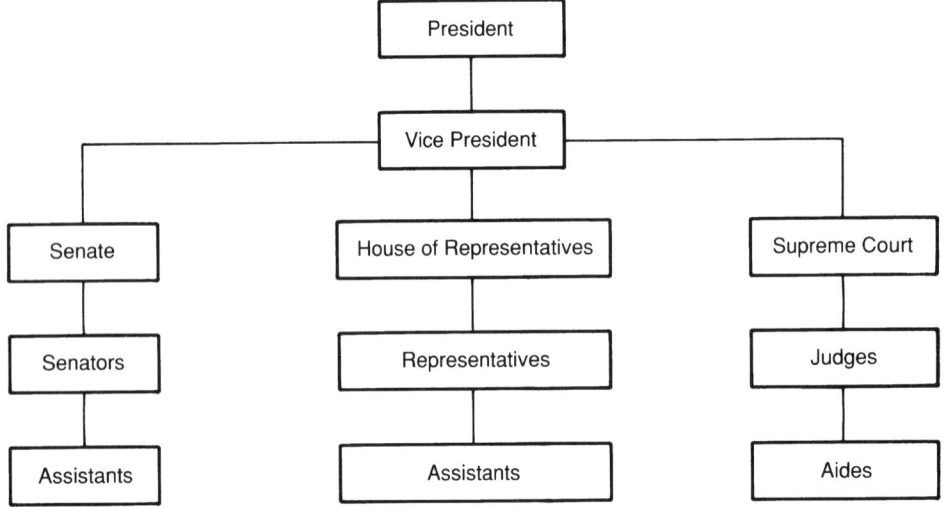

1. Who is the highest ranking official in the United States government?

2. Who works in the Senate?

3. Who works in the House of Representatives?

4. Who works in the Supreme Court?

5. What official is directly below the president?

6. Where do aides work?

7. For whom do assistants work?

Time Lines   4-8

A **time line** shows the relationship between events over time. It also shows when important events happened. Most time lines run from left to right. The left-hand side of the time line is the earliest time and the right-hand side is the latest time. Use the time line to answer the questions.

Major Events of the U.S. Civil War

1861	1862	1863	1864	1865
Civil War begins as Confederates fire on Fort Sumter	Ironclad ships Monitor and Merrimac battle	Battle of Gettysburg won by Union Army	Grant named Commander	Confederates surrender

1. What is the title?

2. What time period is shown?

3. In what time periods is the time line divided?

4. What was the first major event?

5. The last?

6. In what year did the battle of Gettysburg occur?

7. What event occurred the year before the battle of Gettysburg?

8. In what year did the Civil War begin? End?

Diagrams are drawings of objects and their parts. The parts are sometimes labeled on the diagram. Other times the parts are identified in a key that accompanies the diagram. Use the diagram to answer the questions.

Structure of the Human Brain

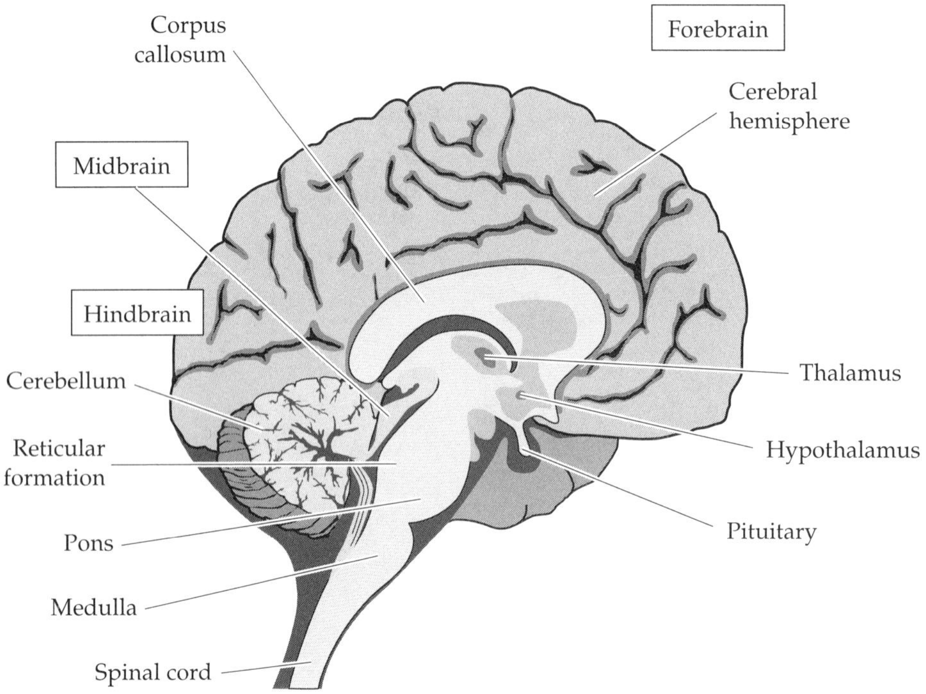
Corpus callosum
Forebrain
Cerebral hemisphere
Midbrain
Hindbrain
Cerebellum
Reticular formation
Pons
Medulla
Spinal cord
Thalamus
Hypothalamus
Pituitary

1. What is the title of this diagram?

2. What can you learn from this diagram?

3. What are the three major structures of the brain?

4. Which of these structures would you find in the back of your head?

5. What connects the medulla to the rest of the body?

6. Is the pituitary closer to the hypothalamus or the cerebellum?

Political and Physical Maps

4-10

A **political map** has lines that show political or government boundaries. Look at the political map of South America, which shows the countries on this continent.

A **physical map** shows the features of the earth's surface such as mountains, highlands, plateaus, deserts, and major bodies of water. Look at the physical map of South America and find these features. No political boundaries are shown.

Political Map of South America

Physical Map of South America

Use the political and physical maps of South America to answer these questions.

1. What countries border Suriname?

2. What mountains border Chile and Argentina?

3. What highlands are north of the Amazon River?

    South?

4. Which two countries in South America are landlocked (no borders on an ocean)?

Copyright © 1999 by Allyn and Bacon.

105

Data Maps

4-11

Data maps are used to show information and data about something for a geographical region. The following data map shows the changes in population across the United States for the period 1960–1990. Use the map and map legend to answer the questions. For some questions you may need to refer to a political map of the United States.

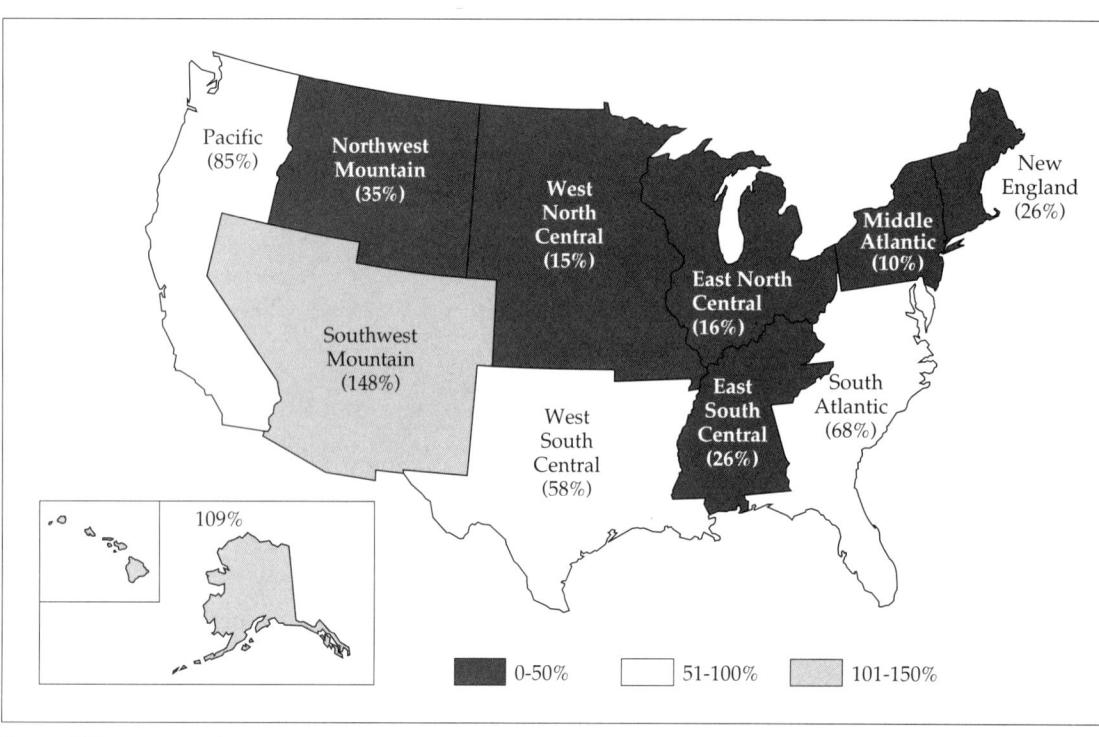

Source: U.S. government.

1. Which section of the United States had the most rapid growth rate in population over the past 30 years?

2. What states had a growth rate of 16%?

3. Which section has had the slowest growth?

4. What was the growth rate in Hawaii and Alaska?

5. Which section has had the higher population growth rate?
   - East North Central or West North Central?
   - South Atlantic or West South Central?
   - New England or Pacific?

Answer Key

4-1 1. American.   2. 1.2 pounds. 7.9 pounds.   3. No.   4. American, Cheddar, and Swiss cheese.   5. U.S. Department of Agriculture. Economic Research Service. *Food Consumption, Prices, and Expenditures, 1996: Annual Data, 1970–1994, Statistical Bulletin* No. 928, April 1, 1996.

4-2 1. Maine.   2. Hawaii.   3. 61.8%.   4. .4%.   5. U.S. Bureau of the Census, *Current Housing Report*, Series H111/95-A.

4-3 Females.   2. 1,824,000. 955,000.   3. 974,000.   4. 43.48%.   5. *Source*: U.S. National Center for Education Statistics. *Digest of Education Statistics*, annual.

4-4 1. Microcomputer software sales in 1994.   2. Types of software.   3. Sales in millions of dollars.   4. Word processors.   5. Finance.   6. Entertainment.   7. About 950 million dollars.

4-5 1. Federal government receipts, outlays, deficits.   2. Increased.   3. Increased.   4. Increased.   5. Decreased.   6. Approximately $175 billion.

4-6 1. Chemical elements in the human body.   2. Oxygen.   3. Carbon.   4. 83%.   5. Carbon.   6. 75%.   7. 100%.   8. Because it is difficult to show very small parts.

4-7 1. President.   2. Senators and assistants.   3. Representatives and assistants.   4. Judges and aides.   5. Vice-president.   6. Supreme Court.   7. Senators and representatives.

4-8 1. Major Events of the U.S. Civil War.   2. 1861–1865.   3. One year.   4. Confederates fire on Fort Sumter and war begins.   5. Confederates surrender.   6. 1863.   7. Battle between the Monitor and the Merrimac.   8. 1861, 1865.

4-9 1. Structure of the human brain.   2. The individual structures/parts that make up the human brain.   3. Forebrain, midbrain, hindbrain.   4. Hindbrain.   5. Spinal cord.   6. Hypothalamus.

4-10 1. French Guiana, Guyana, Brazil.   2. Andes Mountains.   3. Guiana. Brazilian.   4. Bolivia, Paraguay.

4-11 1. Southwest Mountain.   2. East North Central.   3. Middle Atlantic.   4. 109%.   5. East North Central, South Atlantic, Pacific.

CHAPTER FIVE

Using the Internet

CHAPTER OBJECTIVES

1. Teach students to locate different kinds of information on the Internet.
2. Teach students to use effective computer search techniques when looking for information on the World Wide Web (WWW).

TITLES OF REPRODUCIBLE ACTIVITIES

5-1 A Strategy for Using Information Literacy Skills
5-2 Learning about the Internet
5-3 Learning about E-mail
5-4 Advanced E-mail
5-5 Using E-mail
5-6 Practicing Netiquette
5-7 Learning about the World Wide Web
5-8 Using URLs on the WWW
5-9 Tourist Attractions to Explore on the WWW
5-10 Schools to Explore on the WWW
5-11 Libraries to Explore on the WWW
5-12 Reference Sources on the WWW
5-13 Government Sources on the WWW
5-14 Primary Sources on the WWW
5-15 Learning about Your Local FreeNet
5-16 Using Your Local FreeNet
5-17 Learning about Search Engines and Directories
5-18 Using a Search Engine or Directory
Answer Key

USING THE REPRODUCIBLE ACTIVITIES

Use activities 5-1 and 5-2 to introduce students to the Internet. Use activities 5-3 through 5-6 to teach students about e-mail and netiquette, and to provide students with opportunities to use their local e-mail systems. Use activities 5-7 and 5-8 to introduce students to the World Wide Web (WWW). Activities 5-9 through 5-14 provide places to visit using specific URLs. Use activities 5-15 and 5-16 to teach students about FreeNets. Activities 5-17 through 5-19 introduce search engines and directories as search tools for the WWW and provide practice in using them. For activities about evaluating information found on the WWW, see Chapter Six.

5-1 A Strategy for Using Information Literacy Skills

This activity is a modification of 1-1. Use the page to review the definition of information literacy. Have students read the information about the library and the Internet. Then refer students to the flowchart to review the difference between information found on web pages and in books, magazines, and other materials found in a library. Have students write a paragraph that summarizes their experiences in using the library and the Internet to find information. Have students share what they wrote.

5-2 Learning about the Internet

Have students read the introductory text that defines the Internet and explains the different services available on the Internet. Clarify any terms or concepts students do not understand. Have students write what each abbreviation or term represents. Then have students answer the questions about Internet access at their school. You may have students find the answers to these questions in informational material produced by the school and library, or include the answers in a lecture after which the students can answer the questions.

5-3 Learning about E-mail

Review the introductory text describing e-mail. Help students understand how e-mail is used to send and receive messages. Then have students answer the questions. Finally, explain how e-mail can be used to send a message to the President of the United States. Have students write their message to the President.

5-4 Advanced E-mail [C]

Use this activity only if you want to teach a specific e-mail system used by students in your school. Explain the introductory text describing the different e-mail systems. Tell students about the e-mail system used by your school. Ask students to describe e-mail systems they use at home. Then have students complete the activity by performing the various advanced e-mail functions using the e-mail system in your school.

5-5 Using E-mail [C]

Use this activity to reinforce basic e-mail functions for the e-mail system used by your students. Be sure that students have an e-mail account and know how to access their e-mail system before using this activity. Then assign each student an e-mail "buddy" who will be his or her partner for composing and sending e-mail messages in this activity. Provide students with your e-mail address as well as the e-mail addresses of their classmates. Clarify any differences in terminology used by your e-mail system (e.g., is the distribution list an address book?). Finally, have students complete the activity either on their own or in a lab with your assistance.

5-6 Practicing Netiquette

Review the term *netiquette* with students and have them read the guidelines provided.

Explain terms and concepts as needed. Then have students complete the activity by reading the sample e-mail message and completing the two tasks.

If students have access to the WWW, you may extend this activity by directing students to visit one of the listed web sites to learn more about netiquette.

5-7 Learning about the World Wide Web

Use this activity if you want to introduce web pages to your students but do not have a teaching laboratory for them to search the WWW on their own. You can also use this activity if you want to introduce students to web pages before they use computers to search the WWW.

Have students read the introductory text. Clarify terms or concepts as needed. Review the information provided on the Project EASI web page. Point out that web pages vary considerably. Have students answer the questions about the Project EASI web page. Encourage students to bring in examples of other web pages to share with the class.

USING THE INTERNET **111**

5-8 Using URLs on the WWW

Use this activity only if students have access to the WWW. Students may complete the activity either on their own, or in a lab with your assistance. Have students read the introductory text defining a URL. Explain that web browsers vary and that the place to type the URL, or the label for the box where it must be typed, may vary. Then have students complete the activity by typing in the URLs provided and answering the two questions that follow.

You may extend this activity by providing other detailed URLs for students to enter. You may also extend this activity by showing students how to bookmark the sites, explaining that it will save them from typing the URL the next time.

5-9 Tourist Attractions to Explore on the WWW

Use this activity only if students have access to the WWW. Students may complete the activity either on their own, or in a lab with your assistance. Have students select one of the sites to visit on the WWW. Instruct students to complete the activity by surfing the site and reading, synthesizing, and summarizing important information they find. Remind students to apply what they have learned about navigating a web site.

You may extend this activity by asking students to apply the START criteria for evaluating information (activity 6–4).

5-10 Schools to Explore on the WWW

Use this activity only if students have access to the WWW. Students may complete the activity either on their own, or in a lab with your assistance. Have students select one of the sites to visit on the WWW. Explain to students that these are "jump sites" that list additional sites to visit. Instruct students to complete the activity by selecting one school to visit and to read, synthesize, and summarize important information they find. Remind students to apply what they have learned about navigating a web site.

You may extend this activity by asking students to apply the START criteria for evaluating information (activity 6-4).

5-11 Libraries to Explore on the WWW C

Use this activity only if students have access to the WWW. Students may complete the activity either on their own or in a lab with your assistance.

Have students select one of the sites to visit on the WWW. Explain to students that these are "jump sites" that list additional sites to visit. Instruct students to complete the activity by selecting one library to visit and to read, synthesize, and summarize important information they find. Explain to students that most libraries allow the user to access their online catalog from their web page. Tell students that they can usually find out about the online catalog by reading the information on the library's home page. Remind students to apply what they have learned about navigating a web site.

You may extend this activity by asking students to apply the START criteria for evaluating information (activity 6-4).

5-12 Reference Sources on the WWW

Use this activity only if students have access to the WWW. Students may complete the activity either on their own or in a lab with your assistance. Review with students what they learned about reference sources in Chapter Three. Have students complete the activity by going to each reference source on the WWW and describing it.

You may extend this activity by asking students to apply the START criteria for evaluating information (activity 6-4).

5-13 Government Sources on the WWW

Use this activity only if students have access to the WWW. Students may complete the activity either on their own or in a lab with your assistance. Review with students what they learned about government documents in Chapter Two. Explain to students that the WWW is a good place to find information published by government sources because government agencies want to provide broad access to their information at no cost to the user. Explain the three directory sites, each for a different level of government, provided in the activity. Have students complete the activity. Point out that "hints" to follow are provided for some of the questions.

You may extend this activity by asking students to apply the START criteria for evaluating information (activity 6-4).

5-14 Primary Sources on the WWW

Use this activity only if students have access to the WWW. Students may complete the activity either on their own or in a lab with your assistance. Review with students what they learned about primary sources in Chapter Two. Explain to students that the WWW is a good place to find primary

USING THE INTERNET **113**

sources because most of the materials are owned by the library and there are no copyright problems to resolve when scanning the materials.

Have students complete the activity by visiting the American Memory Project at the Library of Congress. Explain that they must follow the steps provided in the activity to locate the full text of the autobiography of Thomas James, a former slave. They must also follow the steps provided to locate photographs of Hopi Indians.

You may extend this activity by providing URLs for other digital library projects that publish primary sources, or online exhibits from special collections departments. You may also extend this activity by asking students to apply the START criteria for evaluating information (activity 6-4).

5-15 Learning about Your Local FreeNet

Explain to students that FreeNets are community-based information systems about a community created by members of the community. Tell students that FreeNets are located in cities and towns all over the world and that they provide free connections to the Internet for everyone in their community. Explain that some FreeNets use a graphical browser but some do not. Finally, explain how FreeNets are a good source of local information.

Review the introductory text with your students. Then have students look at the choices on the sample FreeNet menu and complete the activity.

You can vary this activity by using a menu from your own local FreeNet.

5-16 Using Your Local FreeNet C

Use this activity only if students have access to the WWW. Students may complete the activity either on their own or in a lab with your assistance. Review with students what they learned about FreeNets in 5-15. Then direct students to go to the URL provided and select a FreeNet to visit. Have students complete the activity.

5-17 Learning about Search Engines and Directories C

Use this activity only if students have access to the WWW. Students may complete the activity either on their own, or in a lab with your assistance. Use the text to explain to students the difference between search engines and directories on the WWW. Explain about differences between search engines. Tell students how to find the search feature on the web browser they use. Answer any questions the students may have about search engines and directories. Review computer search techniques covered in Chapter One. Then have students complete the activity.

5-18 Using a Search Engine or Directory [C]

Use this activity only if students have access to the WWW and when they have an assignment that requires them to find information. Review with students Boolean connectors, truncation, proximity, and nesting, covered in Chapter One. Tell students that, just as when using online catalogs and electronic databases, they must develop a search statement when they search for information on the WWW. Then have students complete the activity by developing a search statement for their topic using the rules for the search engine they selected.

A Strategy for Using Information Literacy Skills

5-1

Information literacy is the ability to identify, locate, evaluate and select information in all formats in order to use it effectively. Information literacy expands on basic literacy, which is the ability to read and write, and on computer literacy, the ability to use computers efficiently. To be information literate, you must know how to use the tools and services available in the library and on the Internet. You must also know how to evaluate the information that you find.

The following flowchart shows a strategy for using information literacy skills.

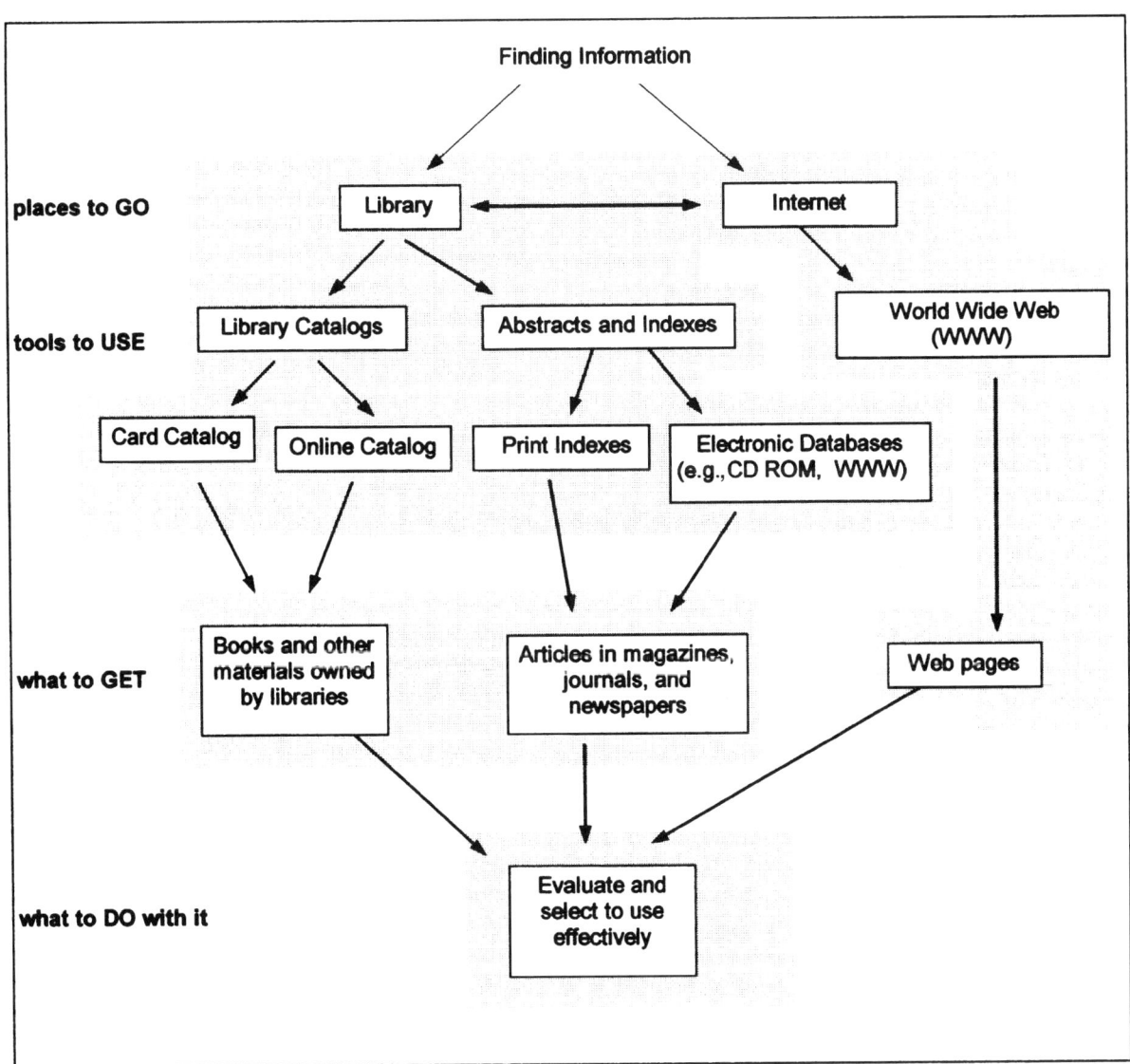

Write a paragraph summarizing your experiences in using the tools and resources in the library and on the Internet to find information.

Copyright © 1999 by Allyn and Bacon.

Learning about the Internet 5-2

The **Internet** is a worldwide network of computers and the cables that connect them. The Internet allows you to use a personal computer to connect to other computers around the world. The Internet is often called the **information superhighway** because this super network is like a road that you can travel to get to information on other computers. The personal computer that you use to connect to the Internet is also called the **client**, and the computers on the Internet with the information on them are called **servers**.

What can you do on the Internet?

- **Electronic mail (e-mail)**: You can use e-mail to send messages to and receive messages from anyone around the world who has a connection to the Internet.
- **Telnet**: Telnet allows one computer to connect to and log on to another computer that is connected to the Internet.
- **File Transfer Protocol (FTP)**: FTP is used to move large files from one computer to another over the Internet. One common use for FTP is to download software from the Internet.
- **Gopher**: Gopher provides a way to browse the Internet by using menus. A gopher site lists options on a menu for you to select and the connections are made over the Internet. Although gophers are being replaced by web pages, it is important to know about them because some information on the WWW is found only on gopher menus.
- **World Wide Web (WWW)**: The WWW is the most common way to search the Internet to find and retrieve information. The information is arranged on web pages stored on computers connected to the Internet. You search the WWW using a browser, software designed to search the Internet. Most web browsers use a graphical user interface (GUI) which means that they can retrieve images in addition to text. Netscape is a popular GUI web browser. Other web browsers are text only. LYNX is a common text-only web browser.

Write what each abbreviation or term stands for:

1. GUI

2. FTP

3. WWW

4. E-mail

Learning about the Internet (continued) **5-2**

Answer these questions about access to the Internet at your school:

5. Can you get your own computer account for the Internet? Do you have to pay for it?

6. List the locations of computers from which you can send/receive e-mail:

7. List the locations from which you can search the WWW using a GUI:

8. Does your computer account allow you to search the WWW from your home? Do you have to pay for it?

9. If you can search the World Wide Web from home with your computer account, does it use a GUI or is it text only?

10. What is the URL for your school's home page?

11. What other useful information did you find out about Internet access at your school?

Learning about E-mail   5-3

You can use e-mail (electronic mail) to send messages to and receive messages from anyone around the world who has a connection to the Internet. You must turn on your computer to send an e-mail message. However, you can receive e-mail in your mailbox even when your computer is turned off.

When you turn on your computer and open your mailbox, you will find any new messages that have been sent to you. There are many different e-mail systems that you can use. They may look very different from each other, but they all provide the same type of service. Here are six things you can do with e-mail.

Send—Send a message.
Read—Read a message.
Delete—Erase a message.
Forward—Send a message to another mailbox.
Reply—Answer the person who wrote you the message.
Print—Print a message.

Think of a reason that you might want to send a message to a student in another state or country.

1. What country or state did you select?

2. Why did you pick this place?

3. What message do you want to send?

You can also use e-mail to send messages to famous people. Here is the URL to send e-mail to the President of the United States:

http://www.whitehouse.gov/WH/Mail/html/Mail_President.html

What would you like to say to the President in an e-mail message? Write your message here:

Advanced E-mail   5-4

There are many different systems you can use for e-mail. Your school may provide one type. You can purchase or download other e-mail programs. Some e-mail systems are web-based. You can use these systems while you are using your web browser. Netscape, for example, includes an e-mail system. Other e-mail systems are based on Telnet. When using e-mail systems based on Telnet, you are logged on to your school (or other host) computer, but you are not using the WWW. All e-mail systems have advanced functions. Some e-mail systems are easier to use than others.

1. What is the name of the e-mail system used in your school?

2. Is the e-mail system at your school part of your web browser? Yes _____ No _____

Advanced E-mail Functions

Managing messages. If you receive many e-mail messages that you want to save, you will want to organize them into folders or files. You can create categories and move the messages into these folders. You can then retrieve and read the messages inside the folders whenever you are logged on.

3. Describe how to create files or folders for messages on your e-mail system:

Creating distribution lists. If you send mail to a group of people regularly, you can create a distribution list that includes all their names. Pick a name for the list and enter all the names and e-mail addresses for the people you want to include. You can then send a message to the list, and it will be sent to everyone on your list.

4. Describe how to create a distribution list for a group of people on your e-mail system:

Sending attachments. Many e-mail systems allow you to attach a file to your message. You can send a word-processing file, a web page, or any other type of file. Sometimes people send attachments in a file format that cannot be read by the receiver. In that case, the message may look like random letters and characters.

5. Describe how to send an attachment on your e-mail system:

Using E-mail 5-5

Perform each of the following functions using your e-mail account. Your instructor will assign you an e-mail buddy with whom you should correspond. ✔ each function as you complete it successfully. Use the space provided to record any notes that you need to remember about performing that e-mail function.

_____ Open your e-mail system and log on to your account.

_____ Compose and send a message to your e-mail buddy.

_____ Copy the message to someone else in your class.

_____ Open and read a message you received.

_____ Reply to a message you received.

_____ Print a message you received.

_____ Create a distribution list for your e-mail buddy, your instructor, and one other person in your class.

_____ Send a message to your distribution list.

_____ Create a folder labeled "Project."

_____ Move all your messages from this assignment into the "Project" folder.

Practicing Netiquette

5-6

Netiquette is a word coined to described etiquette on the Internet ('Net). Netiquette guidelines are unofficial but are generally followed by Internet users. Here are some important netiquette guidelines for you to follow when using e-mail to communicate on the Internet.

Don't SHOUT	❏	"Shouting" means writing your e-mail message in "all caps" (all capital letters). It is generally considered rude to SHOUT YOUR MESSAGE LIKE THIS.
Use "smileys"	❏	"Smileys" such as :-) can be used to convey an emotion that may be difficult to express with just words. There are many different types of smileys you can use. There are websites for lists of smileys and their definitions. One is: http://wellweb.com/behappy/smiley.htm (Do not overuse smileys by putting them everywhere in your message. It can be annoying.)
Use the subject line	❏	Information on the subject line helps readers prioritize their mail. Use the subject line to express the key point of your message. Use a convention such as URG for urgent, or REQ for request before the keyword if you want to clarify the type of e-mail you are sending. For more information see: http://www.webfoot.com/advice/email.context.html?Email
Quote carefully	❏	Do not quote the entire original message in your reply. Select enough of the quote so that your response is clear, but do not waste the reader's time and e-mail disk space by including the entire original message.
No private messages	❏	Remember that e-mail is not private. It may be read by people other than the recipient. It also may be forwarded without your knowledge or consent (a netiquette no-no).
Be concise	❏	Limit messages to fewer than 25 lines and limit lines to 75 characters. Different e-mail systems wrap the lines at different points. Your message can be cut off or may display incorrectly if the lines are too long.
Never "flame"	❏	A "flame" is an insulting or offensive message. You should never flame someone.
Don't "spam"	❏	"Spamming" means sending the same message to a large group of people who did not ask for it. It is considered rude to spam, and you may be flamed for it.

5-6 Practicing Netiquette (continued)

1. Here is an e-mail message. Circle those parts that break netiquette guidelines.

```
To:     All students at Pineview School
From:   Jimmy Brandol
Re:     READ THIS!
Date:   September 21, 1998
```

VOTE FOR ME -THE BEST CANDIDATE FOR SCHOOL TREASURER !!! I'M JIMMY AND IF YOU DON'T
KNOW ME I'M RUNNING FOR CLASS TREASURER. I have some great ideas :-) for raising money and I'm good at
math, not like my opponent Michael Barlow :-(HE'S REALLY BAD AT MATH — HE EVEN GOT A D IN MR
P'S CLASS.;-(I WOULDN'T TRUST HIM WITH OUR MONEY, WOULD YOU? Even his
best friend Tom Vale says he's "kind of irresponsible.";-@ That's what I heard, anyway. So VOTE FOR
ME!!! AND YOU'LL GET THE BEST TREASURER THIS SCHOOL EVER HAD!!!:-)

2. At least seven netiquette guidelines were not followed. Write them here.

Here are some resources on the World Wide Web that may help you learn more about netiquette.

A Beginner's Guide to Effective E-mail: A wonderful manual by Kaitlin Duck Sherwood covering topics such as context, page layout, intonation, and gestures. Includes examples.

    URL: www.webfoot.com/advice/email.top.html

Netiquette: A comprehensive, online book (156 pages) by Virginia Shea. Includes a hyperlinked, detailed table of contents for easy navigation.

    URL: www.albion.com/netiquette/book/index.html

Life on the Internet: Netiquette: Lists sites on the WWW related to Netiquette.

    URL: www.screen.com/start/guide/netiquette.html

Learning about the World Wide Web   5-7

You use the WWW to find information located on any of the servers (computers) connected to the Internet. You need a web browser to use the WWW. Some **web browsers** use **GUI** (graphical user interface) to present graphic images in addition to text. Some common web browsers are Netscape and Internet Explorer. Other web browsers present text only. One of the most common text-only browsers is Lynx.

Information on the WWW is found on **web pages**. The first page in a set of web pages is called the **home page**. A collection of web pages from one person or organization is called a **web site**. With a web browser, you jump from one web page to another by clicking on **hyperlinked** words or images. These hyperlinked words or images are connected to other web pages of related information. Look at the following web page for Project EASI from the U.S. Department of Education.

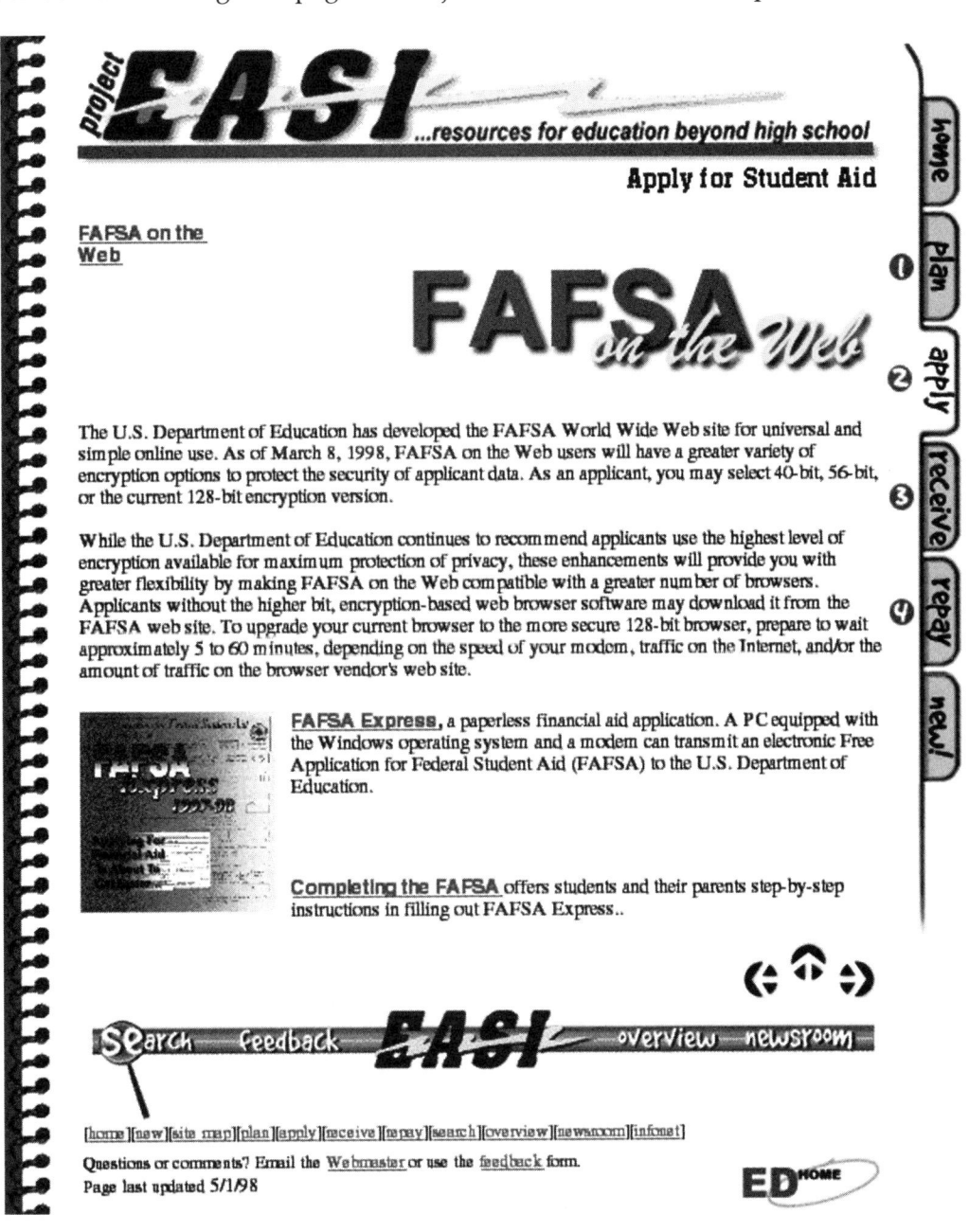

5-7 *Learning about the World Wide Web (continued)*

Refer to the sample web page to answer the following questions:

1. The home page usually provides information about the organization or individual who created the web page(s). What organization is responsible for the information on this home page?

2. Many web pages are designed for text browsers as well as graphical browsers. They include hyperlinked buttons and images that can be used by the graphical browsers. The links may be duplicated for text browsers with hyperlinked words or phrases. On the computer screen, hyperlinked words or phrases are highlighted in different colors from the rest of the text. These words or phrases are underlined when printed.

    What are the four steps of the financial aid process represented by both tabs and buttons on the home page?

    Site Map is one of the hyperlinked phrases. What hyperlinked phrase would you select to send a paperless financial aid application?

3. Some web pages have **navigation buttons**, usually at the bottom of the page. Navigation buttons are linked to the home page or other related pages. What is the name of the navigation button at the bottom of the page?

4. The bottom of a web page often provides information about the page itself, such as who created it, the number of visitors, when it was last updated, and e-mail addresses. What options are provided on this page for sending questions or comments by e-mail?

5. Some larger web sites provide the option to "search" the collection of web pages by keywords. Is there a search option for the Project EASI web site?

Using URLs on the WWW   5-8

An address on the WWW is called the URL (Uniform Resource Locator). If you know the URL for a web page, type it in a web browser to go to that web page. After you press the ENTER key, the Internet will connect your computer with the computer where the information for that web page is located. Look at the sample screen for a web browser to see where the URL is typed.

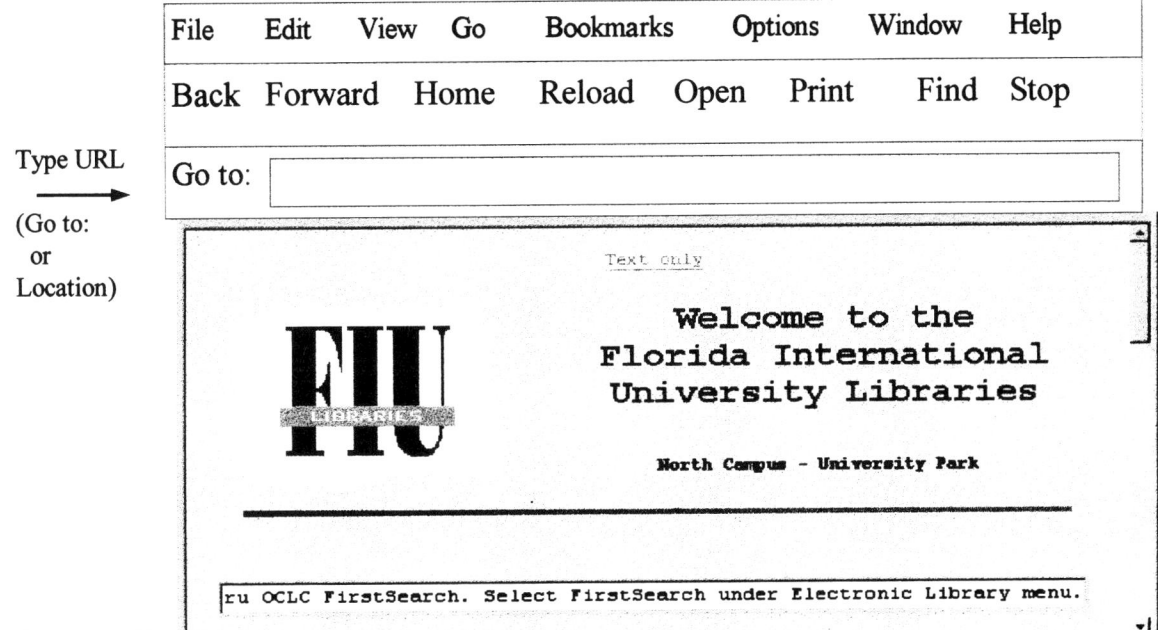

Type URL → (Go to: or Location)

You must type the URL *exactly* as you see it! Follow these rules.

- ❏ Type upper case and lower case letters exactly as given.
- ❏ Include _ or / or ~ or . or % or - exactly as given.
- ❏ Do not add any extra spaces or dots (periods).

1. Type the following URL:

    http://www.mindspring.com/~zoonet/www_virtual_lib/zoos.html

    What is the name of the web page you found at this address? Write it here.

2. Type the following URL:

    http://duke.usask.ca/%7Escottp/free.html

    What is the name of the web page you found at this address? Write it here.

Copyright © 1999 by Allyn and Bacon.

Tourist Attractions to Explore on the WWW   5-9

Here is a list of tourist attractions, museums, and other places you might like to visit. Type in the URLs to visit one or more of them on the WWW.

Metropolitan Museum of Art

> http://www.metmuseum.org

NASA/Kennedy Space Station

> http://www.ksc.nasa.gov/ksc.html

Louvre

> http://www.paris.org/Musees/Louvre/

National Baseball Hall of Fame and Museum

> http://www.baseballhalloffame.org/index.html

Smithsonian Museum

> http://www.si.edu/newstart.htm

Write a paragraph describing something special about one of the places you visited on the WWW. Include facts, data, and statistics that you located on the web pages for this site.

Schools to Explore on the WWW   5-10

Here is a list of schools that you can explore on the WWW. Each of these URLs lists many schools to visit.

K–12 Schools on the WWW

    http://web66.coled.umn.edu/schools.html

U.S. Universities and Community Colleges on the WWW

    http://www.utexas.edu/world/univ/

Select one school to explore. Write a paragraph describing something interesting you learned when you "visited" the school on the WWW. Include facts, data, and statistics about the school that you found interesting and informative.

Libraries to Explore on the WWW   5-11

Here is a list of libraries that you can explore on the WWW. Each of these URLs lists many libraries to visit. In addition to general information about the library, most library web pages include connections to their online catalogs.

School Libraries on the Web

>http://www.cusd.chico.k12.ca.us/~pmilbury/slib.html

Public Libraries on the Web

>http://sunsite.berkeley.edu/Libweb/usa-pub.html

Academic Libraries on the WWW

>http://sunsite.Berkeley.edu/Libweb/usa-acad.html

Select one library to explore. Write a paragraph describing something interesting you learned when you "visited" the library on the WWW. Include information about the library's online catalog.

Reference Sources on the WWW   5-12

Most reference sources such as encyclopedias, dictionaries, and almanacs are published by commercial publishers and are not available on the WWW for free. Some, however, are made available for free on the WWW. Here are some URLs for reference sources on the WWW. Visit each URL and write a concise description of the reference source found.

1. Web of Online Dictionaries

    http://www.bucknell.edu/~rbeard/diction.html

2. Webopaedia

    http://www.pcwebopaedia.com/

3. Statistical Abstract of the United States

    http://www.census.gov/statab/www

4. Acronyms

    http://www.ucc.ie/acronyms/

5. Roget's Thesaurus

    http://humanities.uchicago.edu/forms_unrest/ROGET.html

Government Sources on the WWW

5-13

Government information is one of the most reliable and abundant categories of information available on the WWW. The U.S. federal government makes as much information as possible available at no cost to the user. Many local and state governments also use the WWW to publish their documents. International organizations also publish information on web sites. Here are some good places to start to look for government information.

Federal Web Locator: Includes links to U.S. federal web sites for legislative, executive, and judicial branches of government as well as other federal agencies, commissions, and committees.

> http://www.law.vill.edu/fed-agency/fedwebloc.html

Yahoo—Government—U.S. States: Comprehensive collection of resources arranged by state with a searchable index.

> http://www.yahoo.com/Government/U_S__Government/U_S__States

International Organizations: Includes links to international organizations and their publications, such as the United Nations, the World Bank, NATO, and OECD. Also includes links to non-U.S. governments.

> http://www.library.nwu.edu/govpub/idtf/igo.html

Each of the following questions can be answered by starting at one of the URLs listed above. Select the appropriate starting place and use the hints to answer each question. Write the URL for the page where the question can be answered.

1. Where can you find news releases about world hunger from the World Food Programme, which is a United Nations agency?

2. What is the date and topic of the most recent news release from the World Food Programme?

3. Where can you find information about President's Clinton's Welfare to Work Program? (*Hint:* Follow the links: Under Executive Agency—U.S. Department of Labor, Employment and Training Administration)

4. Where can you find fishing information for South Dakota, including the cost of a fishing license. (*Hint:* Follow the links: South Dakota—Department of Game, Fish, and Parks—Fishing Information—Fishing License Information)

Primary Sources on the WWW

5-14

Primary sources such as diaries, letters, journals, photographs, postcards, and other manuscript materials are often owned by libraries. These manuscript collections are "published" on the WWW in order to make them available to people around the world. In many cases, the images are scanned in for viewing. Often you can find these online collections by visiting the home pages of large libraries.

The American Memory Project, one of the largest projects to publish primary source materials, is under construction at the Library of Congress. This project is a collection of documents, photographs, movies, and sound recordings about American history that will take years to complete. You can visit the Library of Congress on the WWW and use the thousands of items already available in the American Memory Project.

Follow these steps to locate primary source materials at the Library of Congress. ✔ as you complete each step.

_____ 1. Visit the American Memory: Historical Collections for the National Digital Library at http://lcweb2.loc.gov/ammem/

_____ 2. From the home page, select *documents*.

_____ 3. Scroll to *Book and Pamphlet Collections*, and select *African-American Perspectives*.

_____ 4. Browse by subject and select *slave narratives*.

_____ 5. Find the full text of the autobiography by a former slave named Thomas James from 1887. The first sentence of his book tells where he was born. Where was it?

Now complete the following steps to find photographs in the American Memory Project.

_____ 6. Go to the American Memory Project Home Page.

_____ 7. Select *Photos and Prints*.

_____ 8. Search by keyword.

_____ 9. Use the keyword *Hopi* to find images of Hopi Indians.

_____ 10. Describe the pictures that you find.

Learning about Your Local FreeNet

5-15

A FreeNet is a computer information system for your town or city. There are FreeNets throughout the United States and all over the world. FreeNets provide a free connection to the Internet. This connection may allow you to send and receive e-mail and to search for information on the WWW.

Here is a sample FreeNet page from the WWW.

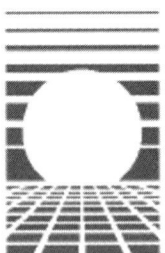

SEFLIN Free-Net
Southeast Florida Library Information Network, Inc.

[Free-Net Registration & User Information | New Items & Training]
[Adding Your Information | Make SEFLIN Free-Net Your Home Page]

Arts & Entertainment
Education & Schools
Home, Garden & Daily Living
Libraries & Literature
News and Media Resources
Science & Technology
Special Interest Groups
Youth - Kids & Teens

Business, Money & Taxes
Government & Communities
Legal, Crime & Safety
Medicine & Health
Religion & Philosophy
Social Services
Sports, Recreation & Travel
Other Free-Nets & Beyond

The SEFLIN Free-Net is sponsored, operated, and governed by the Southeast Florida Library Information Network [SEFLIN], a non-profit organization of libraries in Broward, Dade, Palm Beach, Martin & Monroe counties.

THANKS! to our community [Sponsors & Supporters] for their support in making the Free-Net truly a community resource 'By the People -- For the People'.

Index & Internet Search Tools | HELP

SEFLIN Menu = ([   ]) [Now]

Thanks to SEFLIN Free-Net Supporter: *Martin County Public Library System*

Learning about Your Local FreeNet (continued) **5-15**

Refer to the sample FreeNet page. Write the hyperlinked phrase you would select to do each of the following.

1. Find out what the mayor is planning.

2. Get the home schedule for a local sports team.

3. Get some tax information.

4. Find out about local crime watch groups.

5. Connect to library online catalogs.

6. Find out what films are showing in your town or city

7. Connect to a FreeNet in another city.

8. Find out about your local high schools.

9. Find some information about diets and nutrition.

10. Find out about local services for the homeless.

Using Your Local FreeNet

5-16

Complete this activity to find and explore a FreeNet. Here is the URL for a list of FreeNets located around the world. Use the WWW to go to this web site and select a FreeNet to visit.

http://www.lights.com/freenet/

The FreeNets on the WWW will have (www) after their names. Some may be available only via Telnet or gopher. Select a Freenet to visit and complete the following about the FreeNet you selected.

1. What is the name of the FreeNet you selected?

2. Where is it located?

3. Did you connect by WWW or Telnet?

4. Describe the logon procedure for the FreeNet you selected:

5. Write a concise description of the local community that you selected:

6. What interesting information about this community is available on their FreeNet?

Learning about Search Engines and Directories

5-17

Search engines are computer programs designed to search web pages. The search engine creates a file of web pages that can be searched by keyword. Most search engines offer keyword/Boolean searching. Some common search engines for the WWW are: AltaVista, HOTBOT, WebCrawler, and AOL Netfind.

Here are three things to consider when using a search engine:

- ✔ What is the scope of the WWW covered? Because search engines create a database of web pages for you to search, you are only searching a portion of the WWW. Some search engines are more comprehensive than others.

- ✔ What are the specific search features? Almost all search engines use search strategies that include keywords, Boolean connectors, proximity, and truncation.

- ✔ How are the results displayed? Search engines display their results in different ways. Some show the relevance of the result with a numerical relevance ranking. Others have a rating system.

Directories, sometimes called web guides, are collections of web pages organized by topic. The topics are presented hierarchically, and the user can browse subject lists. The most common directory on the WWW is Yahoo. Others include Lycos, Infoseek, and Excite.

Two things to consider when using Yahoo or any other directory are:

- ✔ An individual or individuals organized the web sites into categories. You will need to browse through the hierarchy of categories to find the information you need.

- ✔ Some directories have a search engine for that site. They allow you to search web pages on that site by keyword.

Most web browsers provide connections to the commonly used search engines and directories. For example, Netscape has a "Net Search" button on its task bar that provides a direct link to a Netscape page that includes various search engines and directories. Microsoft's Internet Explorer has a "Search the Internet" icon that links to a page of search engines and directories.

To learn how the search engine or directory you are using searches for and displays results, read about it by clicking on "Tips" or "Advanced Searching" or "About" or "How to Search." These are some of the terms used on search engines and directories to connect you to pages of detailed information.

For a quick description of some common search engines and directories, see Microsoft's site, "Choosing a Search Service," at: http://www.msn.com/search/choosear.asp?frame=0

5-17 *Learning about Search Engines and Directories (continued)*

Answer the following:

1. Describe how your web browser links to search engines.

2. List the names of all the search engines you can find by using your web browser.

3. Use the Microsoft URL cited above to describe the difference between Excite and AltaVista.

Select one of the search engines or directories listed below and answer the following questions about it.

Search engines: AltaVista   Excite   HOTBOT   WebCrawler   InfoSeek   Lycos

4. Which did you select?

5. What did you learn about the scope of the WWW covered?

6. Does your search engine or directory use the Boolean connectors: AND, OR, NOT? Does it use the words or symbols?

7. How do you search for a phrase (or proximity)?

8. What is the truncation symbol?

9. Can you search for the exact word only or will pages with related terms be retrieved?

10. Does your search engine or directory have a reviewing system where sites or pages are rated?

11. How are the search results displayed?

Using a Search Engine or Directory   5-18

Search engines and directories on the WWW use keywords, Boolean connectors, truncation, proximity, and other search techniques for finding specific information. Use this activity to develop a search strategy for a search engine or directory on the WWW.

1. Review your papers, projects, class presentations and other assignments. Select one that requires you to do research and complete the following:

    I need to find information about the topic:

Underline words in your topic that you can use as keywords. Write these keywords on the chart. Write other forms of the keywords as well as synonyms and related terms.

	1	2	3
Keywords			
Other Forms of Keyword			
Synonyms and Related Terms			

2. Select a search engine or directory to look for information on your topic on the WWW. Read any information provided about how to use that search engine. Develop a search strategy for your topic. Use Boolean connectors, phrase searching, truncation, and any other search features supported by the search engine you selected. Write your search statement for the search engine or directory you selected here.

    Search Statement:

Answer Key

5-1 Paragraphs will vary.

5-2 1. Graphical user interface. 2. File transfer protocol. 3. World Wide Web. 4. Electronic mail. 5. through 11. Answers will vary.

5-3 Answers will vary.

5-4 Answers will vary, but you could provide the correct answers for the e-mail system used at your school.

5-5 All options should be checked as the student completes each task.

5-6 1. To: (All students at Pineview School)
From: Jimmy Brandol
Re: (READ THIS!)
Date: September 21, 1998

(VOTE FOR ME) -THE BEST CANDIDATE FOR SCHOOL TREASURER !!! I'M JIMMY AND IF YOU (DON'T)
KNOW ME I'M RUNNING FOR CLASS TREASURER. I have some great ideas (:-) for raising money and I'm good at
math, not like my opponent Michael Barlow :-(HE'S REALLY BAD AT MATH — HE EVEN GOT A D IN MR
P'S CLASS.;-((I WOULDN'T TRUST HIM WITH OUR MONEY, WOULD YOU?) Even (his)
(best friend Tom Vale says he's "kind of irresponsible.");-@ That's what I heard, anyway. So VOTE FOR
ME!!! AND YOU'LL GET THE BEST TREASURER THIS SCHOOL EVER HAD!!!:-)

2. "Spammed" by sending the message to the entire school.
Subject line is too vague, it does not express the key point of the message.
Sentences are too long so they wrap incorrectly.
Too many different kinds of smileys are used.
SHOUTING by writing in all caps is rude.
The message is offensive to Michael Barlow, his opponent.
A private comment from the opponent's friend is shared with everyone.

5-7 1. Project EASI (from the U.S. Department of Education). 2. plan, apply, receive, repay. FAFSA Express. 3. ED HOME. 4. Contact the Webmaster or use the feedback form. 5. Yes.

5-8 1. The WWW Virtual Library: Zoos. 2. FreeNets and Community Networks.

5-9 Paragraphs will vary.

5-10 Paragraphs will vary.

5-11 Paragraphs will vary.

5-12 Descriptions will vary.

5-13 1. http://www.wfp.org/Pub_Info_PressRel_Home.html 2. Date and topic of most recent issue will depend on date accessed. 3. http://wtw.doleta.gov 4. http://www.state.sd.us/state/executive/gfp/fishing/fish-lic.htm

5-14 1–4. All steps should be checked. 5. Steps should be checked. Canajoharie (New York). 6–9. All steps should be checked. 10. Answers must be one of the following: Hopi woman making pottery; Hopi basket weaver; Hopi mending moccasins; A Hopi cornfield; "The man with the hoe."

5-15 1. Government & Communities. 2. Sports, Recreation & Travel. 3. Business, Money, & Taxes. 4. Legal, Crime, & Safety. 5. Libraries & Literature. 6. Arts & Entertainment. 7. Other FreeNets & Beyond. 8. Education & Schools. 9. Medicine & Health. 10. Social Services.
5-16 Answers will vary.
5-17 Answers will vary.
5-18 Search strategies will vary.

CHAPTER SIX

Evaluating Information

CHAPTER OBJECTIVES

1. Teach students to use a checklist of criteria for evaluating information they find in the library.
2. Teach students to use an expanded checklist of criteria for evaluating information they find on the World Wide Web.

TITLES OF REPRODUCIBLE ACTIVITIES

6-1 A Checklist for Evaluating Information from Library Sources
6-2 Evaluating Information from Library Sources on a Topic
6-3 Evaluating Information from Library Sources on Your Topic
6-4 A Checklist for Evaluating Information from the WWW
6-5 Evaluating Information from the WWW on a Topic
6-6 Evaluating Information from the WWW on Your Topic
6-7 Evaluating WWW Sites
6-8 Evaluating More WWW Sites
     Answer Key

USING THE REPRODUCIBLE ACTIVITIES

Activity 6-1 introduces the START checklist for evaluating information from library sources. Use activities 6-2 and 6-3 to teach students how to use the START checklist with library sources. Activity 6-4 introduces the START checklist for evaluating information found on the WWW. Use activities 6-5 and 6-6 to teach students how to use the START checklist with WWW sources. Finally, use activities 6-7 and 6-8 to have students apply what they have learned about evaluating information found on the WWW to evaluate web sites.

6-1 A Checklist for Evaluating Information from Library Sources

Explain to students why they should evaluate information they find in library sources. Ask students to share what they know about evaluating information. Then introduce the START Checklist for Library Sources by having students read the criteria in each category. Clarify any questions students have. Then explain the directions for completing items 1 through 5. Take students through the example and have them complete the activity.

6-2 Evaluating Information from Library Sources on a Topic

Have students apply what they have learned from using the criteria in the START checklist to decide whether they would use the information provided for a paper on "effective weight loss programs." Students must provide reasons supporting their decisions.

6-3 Evaluating Information from Library Sources on Your Topic

Have students select a topic and then locate information on the topic in a popular magazine. Have students apply what they have learned from using the criteria from the START checklist to decide whether they would use the information from the popular magazine for a paper on their topic. Students must provide reasons supporting their decision. Have students repeat the activity using the information from the scholarly journal.

You may extend this activity by providing articles you choose for students to evaluate.

6-4 A Checklist for Evaluating Information from the WWW

Explain to students the importance of evaluating information that they find on the WWW. Ask students to share what they know about information published on the WWW and how it gets there. Then introduce the START Checklist for the WWW. This checklist is expanded slightly from the START Checklist for Library Sources in 6-1 to include some criteria relevant only to web publishing. Have students read the criteria provided on the checklist and discuss each category. Explain the directions for completing items 1 through 5. Take students through the example and have them complete the activity.

6-5 Evaluating Information from the WWW on a Topic

Have students apply what they have learned from using the criteria in the START checklist to decide whether they would use the information provided from the WWW for a paper on "effective weight loss programs." Students must provide reasons supporting their decisions.

6-6 Evaluating Information from the WWW on Your Topic [C]

Use this activity only if students have access to the WWW. Students may complete the activity either on their own, or in a lab with your assistance. Have students select a topic and then locate information on the topic on the WWW. If students have completed 6-3, they may use the topic they selected for 6-3. Have students apply what they have learned from using the criteria from the START checklist to decide whether they would use the information from the WWW for a paper on their topic. Students must provide reasons supporting their decision.

You may extend this activity by having students evaluate information from a second web site they locate or from a web site that you provide.

6-7 Evaluating WWW Sites [C]

Use this activity only if students have access to the WWW. Students may complete the activity either on their own, or in a lab with your assistance. Have students apply what they have learned from using the criteria in the START checklist to decide whether they would use the information provided from the WWW for a paper on the topic provided. Students must provide reasons supporting their decisions.

6-8 Evaluating More WWW Sites [C]

Use this activity only if students have access to the WWW. Students may complete the activity either on their own, or in a lab with your assistance. Use this activity to provide students with additional practice evaluating information found on the WWW. Have students apply what they have learned from using the criteria in the START checklist to decide whether they would use the information provided from the WWW for a paper on the topic provided. Students must provide reasons supporting their decisions.

A Checklist for Evaluating Information from Library Sources

6-1

You should always evaluate information obtained from library sources. **START** is an acronym that will help you remember the five categories of criteria for evaluating information sources. The letters in the acronym stand for:

    Scope   **T**reatment   **A**uthority   **R**elevance   **T**imeliness

Read to familiarize yourself with the five categories of criteria in the START Checklist for Library Sources.

START Checklist for Library Sources

Scope
- ❏ Are all aspects of the topic covered?
- ❏ Is the coverage in depth?
- ❏ Does the information add new or unique information about your topic?
- ❏ Are there visual aids that enhance the text?

Treatment
- ❏ Is the information presented as fact or opinion?
- ❏ Is evidence provided?
- ❏ Are conclusions logical?
- ❏ Is the information supported by footnotes or references?
- ❏ Is the information free from bias?
- ❏ Is the information consistent with information from other sources?

Authority
- ❏ Are the author's qualifications presented?
- ❏ Does the author have an educational background related to the topic?
- ❏ Does the author have other expertise related to the topic?
- ❏ Is the author affiliated with an educational institution or other reputable organization?
- ❏ Does the publisher or publication have a reputation for reliability?

Relevance
- ❏ Does the information address your topic?
- ❏ Does the information provide evidence for your point of view?
- ❏ Does the information verify other information you are using from other sources?

Timeliness
- ❏ Is the information sufficiently current for your purpose?
- ❏ Regardless of the date, is the information still useful?

Copyright © 1999 by Allyn and Bacon.

6-1 *A Checklist for Evaluating Information from Library Sources (continued)*

Use the START checklist to evaluate the information from library sources in items 1 through 5. Follow these directions:

- Read item 1 and decide which category from the START checklist is appropriate for evaluating the information. Write the name of the category on the line provided.
- Write a statement that tells why you decided this is the category that best applies.
- Repeat for each library source in 2 through 5.

Example: *Authority* A magazine article about the dangers of heart bypass surgery written by a person certified in acupuncture.

The issue is whether someone certified in acupuncture is knowledgeable about bypass surgery.

1. _____ A video about current trends in nuclear energy produced in 1968.

2. _____ An article in a magazine published by the National Beef Council about the nutritional value of eating beef.

3. _____ An article in an engineering journal, written by a safety engineer, about the value of safety devices in automobiles.

4. _____ A book presenting scientific information on the creation of the universe for a paper to be written on the topic of the Big Bang theory for a class in astronomy.

5. _____ A newspaper article with the title "Agriculture in the South" that discusses only the growing of cotton.

Evaluating Information from Library Sources on a Topic

6-2

Scope   **T**reatment   **A**uthority   **R**elevance   **T**imeliness

Write **yes**, **no**, or **maybe** in front of each source to indicate whether or not you would use it as a source of information for a paper about **effective weight loss programs**. Use what you have learned from the START checklist to guide you as you make your decision for each source. Explain the reason(s) for each decision.

1. _____ An article in *People* magazine on "Celebrity Diet Fads." The author has a B.A. in English and a master's degree in journalism, and is on the staff of writers for the magazine.

2. _____ An interview on *60 Minutes* with the surgeon general of the United States on "Weight Loss Clinics: The Fooling of America." The surgeon general is an M.D. who had 35 years experience as a doctor and medical researcher before becoming surgeon general.

3. _____ A 1997 article in the *Journal of Consulting and Clinical Psychology* on "The Effectiveness of Behavioral Weight Loss Programs: A Follow-Up Study." The author is a Ph.D. in psychology and a tenured faculty member at a large research university.

4. _____ *The Lose-it Clinic Method: The Only Safe Way to Lose Weight*: A book written by the owner of the Lose-it Clinics, a national chain of weight loss clinics under investigation by the Food and Drug Administration.

5. _____ Paper presented at the Fourth International Conference on Obesity Management about the National Hospital Mental Health Program in France, 1980–1990. The article is written by a psychiatrist on the staff of a major hospital in Paris.

6. _____ 1990 newspaper article in the *New York Times*, "America's Most Popular Weight Loss Programs," written by the food editor.

Evaluating Information from Library Sources on Your Topic

6-3

Scope   **T**reatment   **A**uthority   **R**elevance   **T**imeliness

Review the papers, projects, and class presentations you must do this semester. Select one that requires you to do research to complete the assignment.

Write the topic here:

Popular Magazine

Find information on your topic in a popular magazine. Write the citation for the article here:

Write **yes**, **no**, or **maybe** to indicate whether or not you would use this information from the article for the assignment. Use what you have learned from the START checklist to guide you as you make your decision. Explain the reason(s) for your decision:

Scholarly Journal

Do the same using information from a scholarly journal:

A Checklist for Evaluating Information from the WWW

6-4

You should always evaluate information found on the WWW. **START** is an acronym that will help you remember the five categories of criteria for evaluating information sources found on the WWW. The letters in the acronym stand for:

    Scope   **T**reatment   **A**uthority   **R**elevance   **T**imeliness

Read to familiarize yourself with the five categories of criteria in the START checklist for information found on the WWW.

START Checklist for the WWW

Scope
- ❑ Are all aspects of the topic covered?
- ❑ Is the coverage in depth?
- ❑ Does the information add new or unique information about your topic?
- ❑ Are there visual aids that enhance the text?

Treatment
- ❑ Is the information presented as fact or opinion?
- ❑ Is evidence provided?
- ❑ Are conclusions logical? Are there links to more information or references?
- ❑ Is the information free from bias?
- ❑ Is the information consistent with information from other sources?

Authority
- ❑ Are the author's qualifications presented? Is the page signed?
- ❑ Is there any information about the author available?
- ❑ Does the author have an educational background related to the topic?
- ❑ Does the author have other expertise related to the topic?
- ❑ Is the author affiliated with an educational institution or other reputable organization? Is .edu for "education" part of the URL? Is .gov for "government" part of the URL?
- ❑ Is the information from a web site for an organization that is reliable? Do you know anything about the reputation of the organization? Is there any information on the page about the organization?

Relevance
- ❑ Does the information address your topic?
- ❑ Does the information provide evidence for your point of view?
- ❑ Does the information verify other information you are using from other sources?

Timeliness
- ❑ Is there a date provided for the web page and the information on it?
- ❑ Is the information sufficiently current for your purpose?
- ❑ Regardless of the date, is the information still useful?

6-4 *A Checklist for Evaluating Information from the WWW (continued)*

Use the START checklist to evaluate information from the WWW in items 1 through 5. Follow these directions:

- Read item 1 and decide which category from the START checklist is appropriate for evaluating the information. Write the name of the category on the line provided.
- Write a statement that tells why you decided this is the category that best applies.
- Repeat for each WWW source in 2 through 5.

Example   *Treatment*   Web pages endorsing a new cure for baldness by the company that produces the formula.

The issue is whether or not the information is free from bias because the company stands to profit financially from sales of the formula.

1. _____ Information about the "smokers' rights movement" from the R. J. Reynolds Tobacco Company web pages.

2. _____ Information about current negotiations between Israel and the Palestinians from a web page dated January 1997.

3. _____ A scientific explanation of why snow is white from the Discovery Channel's web pages.

4. _____ The latest video images from Mars from the Sojourner rover found on the NASA web site.

5. _____ Information from the United Nations web site about world famine relief for a paper on world hunger.

Evaluating Information from the WWW on a Topic

6-5

Scope   **T**reatment   **A**uthority   **R**elevance   **T**imeliness

Write **yes**, **no**, or **maybe** in front of each source of web information to indicate whether or not you would use it for a paper about **effective weight loss programs**. Use what you have learned from the START checklist to guide you as you make your decision. Explain the reason(s) for your decision.

1. _____ The text of an interview with a weight loss researcher at a major university found at the web site from a major television network.

2. _____ Information on weight loss found on a web site maintained by a company that sells weight loss products.

3. _____ A research report explaining the benefits of vitamin C in fighting colds on a web site from a scientific organization.

4. _____ A series of pictures found on a web site showing people with slim figures followed by statements endorsing the use of an exercise machine.

5. _____ News reports on research findings relevant to weight loss found on a web site created by a newspaper whose reporter attended the scientific conference where the research findings were announced.

6. _____ A series of personal testimonials from people all using the same weight loss program published.

Copyright © 1999 by Allyn and Bacon.

Evaluating Information from the WWW on Your Topic

6-6

Scope   **T**reatment   **A**uthority   **R**elevance   **T**imeliness

Review the papers, projects, and class presentations you must do this semester. Select one that requires you to do research to complete the assignment.

Write the topic here:

Use a search engine or a directory to find information on your topic on the WWW. Write the author, title, date, and URL for the information here:

Write **yes**, **no**, or **maybe** to indicate whether or not you would use this information from the WWW for the assignment. Use what you have learned from the START checklist to guide you as you make your decision. Explain the reason(s) for your decision:

Evaluating WWW Sites   6-7

You must evaluate information found on the WWW before you select it for use. Your evaluation should be based on the criteria from the **START** checklist for the WWW presented in 6-4.

Scope   **T**reatment   **A**uthority   **R**elevance   **T**imeliness

Go to each of the following web sites. Evaluate the information according to the START criteria. For each web site, use the START criteria to decide if the information found on the web site is useful for the topic provided. Write **yes**, **no**, or **maybe** on the line in front of the web site. Explain the reason(s) for your decision.

1. **Web site**: _____ America's Job Bank

    http://www.ajb.dni.us

    Topic: Employment Outlook and Earnings for Accountants

2. **Web site**: _____ U.S. Department of Energy: Energy Efficiency and Renewable Energy Network

    http://www.eren.doe.gov

    Topic: Earth Sheltered Housing

3. **Web site**: _____ National Organization for Women Home Page

    http://www.now.org

    Topic: Gay Rights

Copyright © 1999 by Allyn and Bacon.

Evaluating More WWW Sites 6-8

Here are more web sites to evaluate. Use the criteria from the START checklist in 6-4.

Scope   **T**reatment   **A**uthority   **R**elevance   **T**imeliness

Go to each of the following web sites. Evaluate the information according to the START criteria. For each web site, use the START criteria to decide if the information found on the web site is useful for the topic provided. Write **yes**, **no**, or **maybe** on the line in front of the web site. Explain the reason(s) for your decision.

1. **Web site**: _____ Everglades Digital Library

    http://everglades.fiu.edu/library/index.html

    Topic: Are Crocodiles an Endangered Species?

2. **Web site**: _____ National Park Service

    http://www.nps.gov

    Topic: Native American Burial Grounds

3. **Web site**: _____ Project EASI

    http://easi.ed.gov

    Topic: The Cost of a College Education

Answer Key

6-1 Best answers are: 1. *Timeliness*. The issue is whether or not a video produced in 1968 is sufficiently current on the topic of nuclear energy. 2. *Treatment*. The issue is whether or not the information is free from bias since the National Beef Council is interested in promoting the sale of beef. 3. *Authority*. The issue is whether or not a safety engineer has the educational background and expertise to be qualified to write on this topic and if the article appears in an appropriate professional journal. 4. *Relevance*. The issue is whether or not a book presenting evidence on the creation of the universe will include information about the Big Bang theory. 5. *Scope*. The issue is whether or not the article is too limited because it does not cover all aspects of the topic, or if it may contain some useful information.

6-2 Best answers are: 1. Maybe. 2. Yes. 3. Yes. 4. No. 5. No. 6. Maybe. Reasons provided by students will vary but should reflect the criteria in the five START categories.

6-3 Answers will vary.

6-4 Best answers are: 1. *Treatment*. The issue is whether or not the information is free from bias because the tobacco company has a vested interest in supporting the smokers' rights movement. 2. *Timeliness*. The issue is whether or not the information about negotiations between Israel and the Palestinians from 1997 is sufficiently current given the rapid pace of change on this topic. 3. *Authority*. The issue is whether or not the information is from a reliable web site created by an organization with a good reputation. 4. *Scope*. The issue is whether or not images from NASA would provide unique information. 5. *Relevance*. The issue is whether or not information about world famine relief would be relevant for a paper on world hunger.

6-5 Best answers are: 1. Yes. 2. No. 3. No. 4. Maybe. 5. Yes. 6. Maybe. Reasons provided by students will vary but should reflect the criteria in the five START categories.

6-6 Answers will vary.

6-7 Best answers based on the information on the web site are: 1. Yes. 2. Yes. 3. Maybe. Reasons provided by students will vary but should reflect the criteria in the five START categories.

6-8 Best answers based on the information on the web site are: 1. Maybe. 2. Maybe. 3. Yes. Reasons provided by students will vary but should reflect the criteria in the five START categories.

CHAPTER SEVEN

Writing a Research Paper

CHAPTER OBJECTIVES

1. Teach students a strategy for writing a research paper.
2. Teach students how to identify, locate, and document information needed to write a research paper.

TITLES OF REPRODUCIBLE ACTIVITIES

7-1 A Strategy for Writing a Research Paper
7-2 Choosing a Topic
7-3 Informative and Persuasive Topics
7-4 Practice Writing Persuasive Topics
7-5 Focusing Your Research
7-6 Locating Sources of Information
7-7 Preparing Bibliography Cards
7-8 Preparing Note Cards
7-9 Writing the Outline
7-10 Writing the Draft
7-11 Revising the Draft
7-12 Preparing Footnotes
7-13 Preparing the Title Page
7-14 Preparing the Table of Contents
7-15 Preparing the Bibliography
7-16 Final Checklist
     Answer Key

USING THE REPRODUCIBLE ACTIVITIES

Use the activities in this chapter to take students through the steps of writing a research paper. Students should develop their papers as they move through the activities. Use activity 7-1 to introduce the ten steps in a strategy for writing a research paper. Use activities 7-2 through 7-5 to teach students how to select an appropriate informative or persuasive topic. Use activities 7-6 and 7-7 to have students locate information needed for their papers and to document each source on bibliography cards. Use activities 7-8 through 7-15 to show students how to write and revise the paper. Finally, use 7-16 to have students check their paper before they hand it in.

7-1 A Strategy for Writing a Research Paper

Have students take notes as you elaborate on each of the ten steps in writing a research paper. Have students provide the information regarding research papers they must write.

7-2 Choosing a Topic

Use the text and the two examples to help students learn how to choose a topic that is not too broad. Have students complete the activity by narrowing and rewriting the three topics provided. Then have students return to 7-1 and rewrite topics to make them just right.

7-3 Informative and Persuasive Topics

Use the introductory text to explain the difference between informative and persuasive topics. Have students complete the activity.

7-4 Practice Writing Persuasive Topics

Review the example provided and point out how including a point of view changes the informative topic "Competition between Japanese and American automobile manufacturers" to the persuasive topic "Japanese cars are better than American cars." Use this exercise to give students practice rewriting informative topics into persuasive topics.

7-5 Focusing Your Research

Explain the importance of focusing research when writing research papers. Assist students to answer the questions for the topics they have chosen.

7-6 Locating Sources of Information [L] [C]

Use this activity to familiarize students with the process of finding information in various sources. If necessary, quickly review these sources. Students will have to go to the library to complete this activity. Encourage them to look for electronic sources of information such as on CD ROM. Eliminate the web page as a source if students do not have access to the WWW.

7-7 Preparing Bibliography Cards

Explain the importance of using bibliography cards to document sources of information used when writing research papers. Caution students about plagiarism. Tell students they must prepare a separate bibliography card for each source of information, whether print or electronic. Use the sample cards to explain how bibliography cards are prepared for each type of source of information. Point out that for a given information source, the citation may not include all the parts called for on a bibliography card. For example, the author might not be identified in the citation.

Point out that information for bibliography cards for electronic sources comes from the computer record. The headings on a computer record will not necessarily match the headings required for a bibliography card. Students will have to match the information on a computer record with the information needed for a bibliography card.

Have students prepare bibliography cards for the nine types of sources of information found in 7-6.

7-8 Preparing Note Cards

Explain to students why they need to prepare note cards. Have students refer to the sample bibliography card and the note cards that go with it. Tell students that they must follow the five steps as they prepare note cards for their papers. Emphasize the need for legible writing. Remind students to use abbreviations, acronyms, and other brief forms to reduce the amount of text they write. Have students use what they learned to prepare note cards for their papers.

7-9 Writing the Outline

Explain to students why they need to prepare an outline. Have students refer to the sample outline. Tell them that they must follow the seven steps as they prepare outlines for their papers. Have students use what they learned to prepare outlines for their papers.

7-10 Writing the Draft

Tell students they must write a draft of their research papers. Use the text and sample pages to explain the parts of a research paper that must be included in a draft. Point out that not all sections of a research paper are included in a draft. The title page (7-13), table of contents (7-14), and bibliography (7-15) will be added when preparing the final paper.

Have students follow the five steps to write drafts of their research papers. Tell them to double space their drafts to leave room for revisions.

7-11 Revising the Draft

Show students how to use the Revising Checklist to revise their drafts. Have students continue to revise their drafts until they can answer yes to each question on the checklist.

7-12 Preparing Footnotes

Use the introductory text to explain and demonstrate why and how footnotes are prepared. Have students answer the questions. Tell students where you want them to place footnotes in their research papers. Then have them add footnotes to their papers.

7-13 Preparing the Title Page

Use the introductory text and sample title page to explain what a title page contains and how to prepare it. Then have students prepare title pages for their papers, using the format shown or one you prefer.

7-14 Preparing the Table of Contents

Use the introductory text and sample table of contents to explain what a table of contents contains and how to prepare it. Have students prepare tables of contents for their papers.

7-15 Preparing the Bibliography

Use the introductory text and sample bibliography to explain what a bibliography is and how to prepare it. Have students prepare bibliographies for their papers.

7-16 Final Checklist

Discuss with students how to use the Final Checklist and then have students complete the checklist. Help students make any revisions necessary until they can answer yes to all the questions.

A Strategy for Writing a Research Paper 7-1

A **research paper** is a paper that you write in which you cite information from a variety of sources. Research papers always include a bibliography of sources used or consulted. Follow these steps as you organize, write, and document your research paper:

Step 1   Choose a topic.

Step 2   Identify and select sources of information.

Step 3   Prepare bibliography cards to document the sources of information used.

Step 4   Prepare note cards to record information from each source used.

Step 5   Prepare an outline for the research paper.

Step 6   Write and revise drafts of the research paper.

Step 7   Prepare footnotes to give credit to sources from which you quoted or took major ideas.

Step 8   Prepare a bibliography according to the style manual required by your instructor.

Step 9   Prepare a title page and table of contents.

Step 10 Proofread the research paper.

Review your assignments to identify classes for which you have to write a research paper. For each paper, write the name of the class, the topic, and the date the research paper is due.

Class   *Topic*   *Date Due*

Choosing a Topic   7-2

The first step in writing a research paper is to choose a **topic**. If the topic you choose is too broad, there will be too much information available and you may not be able to complete the research paper in the number of pages assigned. Choose a topic that has sufficient information but not so much that you will find it difficult to complete a paper about the topic within the assigned number of pages.

Read each of the following two topics. Each topic is too broad. Read to learn why each is too broad and what can be done to narrow it.

Topic: The popularity of music

This topic is too broad because there are many types of music from many cultures covering the entire history of the human race. To narrow this topic, you could select a specific type of music, such as rock and roll, or a specific perspective, such as history. A better topic would be "the history of rock and roll." This topic is sufficiently focused to complete a paper within a reasonable number of pages.

Topic: Entertainment for children

This topic is too broad because there are so many different forms of entertainment and so many issues related to entertainment. Entertainment needs to be narrowed down to a specific form of entertainment (e.g., video games), and/or to a specific issue related to entertainment (e.g., violence). A better topic would be "violence in video games."

Each of the following topics is too broad. Narrow and rewrite each topic to make it appropriate for a research paper.

1. Exploring space

2. Immigration to the United States

3. Latin American culture

4. Review your topic(s) from 7-1. Where necessary, rewrite each topic that is too broad.

Informative and Persuasive Topics 7-3

When a research paper provides information without the writer's own point of view, it is an **informative** research paper. When the writer presents the information to support a point of view or to argue against an alternative point of view, it is a **persuasive** research paper.

For example, "Homeless children in America" is a topic for an informative paper. "More funding is needed to support the homeless" is a topic for a persuasive paper.

Place **I** in front of topics that suggest an informative research paper, and **P** in front of topics that suggest a persuasive research paper.

1. ____ Current trends in school discipline.

2. ____ Video games should be rated.

3. ____ The driving age should be raised to 18.

4. ____ Violence in video games.

5. ____ Professional football players earn too much.

6. ____ Punishment for graffiti violators should include cleanup.

7. ____ The United States should fund famine relief.

8. ____ Automobile accidents in the United States.

9. ____ School uniforms don't work.

10. ____ Famine in Africa.

11. ____ Recycling efforts in business.

12. ____ How to clean up industrial waste.

13. ____ Salaries for professional athletes.

14. ____ All offices should recycle paper.

Practice Writing Persuasive Topics   7-4

Study the example to learn how an informative topic was changed to a persuasive topic by including a point of view.

Informative: Competition between Japanese and American automobile manufacturers

Persuasive: Japanese cars are better than American cars.

Rewrite each informative topic to make it persuasive.

1. Funding for public schools

2. Censorship on the Internet

3. Welfare and the elderly

4. The message of rap music

5. The Mars voyager mission

6. Cigarette advertising in Europe

7. Capital punishment in the United States

8. Salaries for professional athletes

Focusing Your Research   7-5

Select one of your topics from 7-1 and write it here:

Before you begin to write your paper and search for information, you must be specific about the kind of paper you will write and information you will need. Answering these questions will help you focus your research. Use a ✔ to show your answers.

1. Will this be a paper only, or is there an oral presentation as well?

    Written paper ____

    Written paper and oral presentation/speech ____

2. Which visual aids do you need to include?

    Pictures ____ Photographs ____ Graphs ____ Charts ____ Maps ____

    Other visual aids? Write them here.

3. What should be the length of your paper?

    1 to 5 pages ____ 6 to 10 pages ____ More than 10 pages ____

4. Is your paper informative ____ or persuasive ____?

5. Do you need any historical information? Yes ____ No ____

    Describe what you need:

6. Do you need information from within the last year? Yes ____ No ____

    Describe what you need:

7. Are there terms or concepts associated with this topic that you do not understand?

    Yes ____ No ____ List them:

8. Are there questions that must be answered with numbers or statistics?

    Yes ____ No ____ Write them here:

Locating Sources of Information

7-6

Write the topic you selected in 7-5:

Find information on your topic in the library or on the Internet. Locate as many sources of information as needed to complete your paper. Use at least one source from each of the following categories to obtain information to write your paper. Write the title for one source for each category. Place a ✔ in front of the title for each source that was found in an electronic format. In activity 7-7 you will prepare bibliography cards for these sources.

Encyclopedia

_____ Title:

Other Reference Book

_____ Title:

Popular Magazine

_____ Title:

Newspaper

_____ Title:

Scholarly Journal

_____ Title:

Book

_____ Title:

Government Document

_____ Title:

Audio/Visual

_____ Title

World Wide Web

Title of web page:

Preparing Bibliography Cards 7-7

In a research paper you must give credit to the sources from which you took information. Using information from a source without giving credit is plagiarism. Credit is given by documenting the source of the information in the bibliography you will prepare for your paper.

Bibliography cards are used to keep a record of the sources from which you obtained information for your paper. Examine the sample bibliography cards prepared for a wide variety of sources. Use these as models to create bibliography cards to document the sources you located in 7-6.

Book
Friedlander, Paul. Rock and Roll: A Social History. Boulder, CO: Westview Press, 1996.

Encyclopedia
Coppage, Noel. "Rock Music." Encyclopedia Americana. 1995 ed.

Magazine Article
Chappell, Kevin. "How Blacks Invented Rock and Roll: R & B Stars Created Foundations of Multibillion-dollar Music Industry." Ebony Jan. 1997: 52-54.

Journal Article
Poiger, Uta G. "Rock 'n' Roll, Female Sexuality, and the Cold War Battle over German Identities." Journal of Modern History 68:3 (1996): 577-617.

Government Document
United States. Cong. Senate. Committee on the Judiciary. Subcommittee on Juvenile Justice. Shaping Our Responses to Violent and Demeaning Imagery in Popular Music. Hearing. 103rd Cong., 2nd session. Washington: GPO, 1995.

Newspaper Article
Pareles, Jon, "Finally Reckoning with Rock History. (Concert at the Opening of the Rock-and-Roll Hall of Fame in Cleveland, Ohio)" New York Times 4 Sept. 1995, nat'l ed.:9.

Audio/Visual
Britain Invades, America Fights Back. Written, produced and directed by Andrew Solt. Videocassette. Time-Life Video and Television, 1995

Electronic Database
Author: Aquila, Richard.
Title of Article: "A Scholar Takes His Views on Rock 'n' Roll to the Air."
Title of Publication: Chronicle of Higher Education
Date of Article: Pages: 31 Jan. 1997:B7+.
Title of Database: UMI Periodical Abstracts
Publication Medium: CD ROM
Vendor Location and Name: Ann Arbor, MI: UMI,
Date of Database: 1997.

World Wide Web
Author: Rock and Roll Hall of Fame and Museum
Title: Rockhall.com
Date of Information: 29 July. 1997
Site: Rock and Roll Hall of Fame and Museum.
URL: http://www.rockhall.com
Online Service: World Wide Web, Netscape
Date Accessed: July 29, 1997.

Preparing Note Cards   7-8

Look at the sample bibliography card and the note cards that go with it. **Note cards** are used to write notes or quotes from the source listed on the bibliography card. You must prepare one or more note cards for each bibliography card.

Sample Bibliography Card

```
                                      1
Aquila, Richard. "A Scholar Takes His
Views on Rock n' Roll to the Air"
Chronicle of Higher Education.
43:21(1997): B7.
```

Note Cards

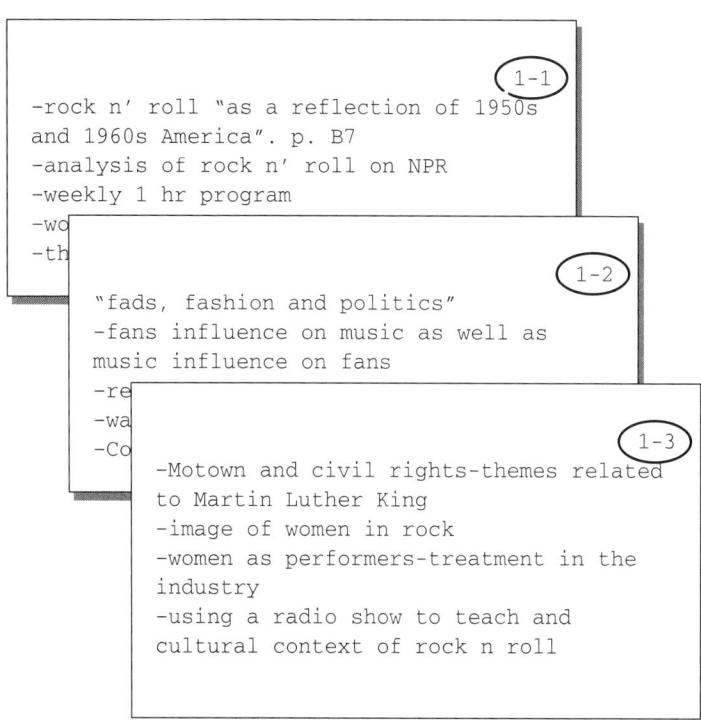

Follow these steps as you prepare note cards for your paper.

Step One Arrange your bibliography cards in alphabetical order by the first word on the card. When alphabetizing, ignore initial articles such as *A*, *An*, or *The*.

Step Two Number your bibliography cards starting with 1 for the first card. Write the number in the upper right-hand corner as in the sample bibliography card. The 1 in the upper right-hand corner of the sample card shows this is the first bibliography card.

Step Three Number your note cards using two numbers separated by a dash as in the sample note cards. Write the number in the upper right-hand corner. In the sample note card numbered 1-1, 1 shows that the notes are for the source listed on bibliography card 1, and -1 shows this is the first card used to record notes from this source. A second note card would be numbered 1-2, and so on.

Step Four Circle the numbers in the upper right-hand corner on the note cards to keep them separate from other numbers you might write when taking notes.

Step Five Write notes on the note cards. Use your own words whenever possible. Place quotation marks around all quotes. Write the page number on which each quote appears.

Writing the Outline   7-9

Look at the sample **outline** for a research paper. It shows how to organize information from your note cards into main topics, subtopics, details, and subdetails.

The History of Rock and Roll

I. The early years
    A. Influence of black music
        1. Rhythm and blues
           a. Clubs in Harlem, Memphis, and Chicago
           b. Early black performers
        2. Church music
    B. The British influence
        1. Beatles
        2. Rolling Stones
        3. The Who
    C. The psychedelic years
        1. Drugs and rock
           a. The acid generation
           b. Songs about drugs
        2. "On the road"
II. Rock and roll and popular culture
    A. Rebellion and rock music
        1. The generation gap
        2. The Vietnam War
    B. Fashion and rock music
    C. Women and rock music
        1. Women artists
        2. Women in song
III. Rock and roll around the world
    A. American culture in Europe
        1. Germany
        2. France
    B. East Asian rock
        1. Japanese rock and roll

Follow these steps as you prepare an outline for your paper.

Step One   Write the title of the research paper.

Step Two   Organize the notes from your note cards into main topics.

Step Three   Write the Roman numeral I and after it the first main topic. Write the Roman numeral II for the second main topic, and so on.

Step Four   Write the subtopics that go with the first main topic. Use capital letters before each subtopic.

Step Five   Write the details that go with each of these subtopics. Use Arabic numerals before each detail.

Step Six   Write the subdetails that go with each of these details. Use small letters before each subdetail.

Step Seven   Repeat steps 4, 5, and 6 for each main topic.

Writing the Draft

7-10

A draft is a paper you write that must be revised before it becomes your final paper. Read about the parts of a research paper that you must include in your draft. Look at the sample pages that show where the parts are located in the research paper. Follow these steps as you write a draft of your research paper.

Step One Write the title at the top of the page. The title is a short statement that tells the subject of your paper.

Step Two Write an introduction that introduces the topic and tells the reader what your paper will be about. The introduction is a paragraph or two at the beginning of a paper.

Step Three Write the body of your paper. It begins after the introduction and ends before the conclusion. The body includes headings and the text that goes with them. The body is the longest part of the paper, usually several pages.

Step Four Insert any pictures, drawings, charts, and other visual aids that will help the reader understand what you are writing about in your paper.

Step Five Write a conclusion. The conclusion tells the reader what you have learned about the topic or summarizes your point of view.

Revising the Draft   7-11

Use the **Revising Checklist** to learn what changes you may need to make in the draft of your paper. Place a ✔ in front of each question for which you can answer yes. Continue to revise your draft until you have a ✔ in front of each question.

Revising Checklist

____ Does the introduction clearly introduce the topic?

____ Did I include headings to help the reader understand the topic?

____ Does the body of the paper contain all facts needed?

____ Does each paragraph contain a main idea?

____ Does each paragraph add something to the paper?

____ Did I choose the best words to explain ideas?

____ Does my conclusion follow from the facts?

____ Did I spell all words correctly?

____ Did I capitalize words correctly?

____ Is there subject–verb agreement in all cases?

____ Are tenses consistent?

____ Are all sentences complete?

____ Did I use quotation marks to identify all quotations?

____ Did I number the pages correctly?

____ Do I have a one-inch margin at the top, bottom, and both sides?

____ Have I reread the paper several times to find ways to improve it?

Preparing Footnotes

7-12

Footnotes are used to document each source of information you use. They provide credit for the source of information. Each footnote is assigned a footnote reference number. The reference footnote number is 1 for the first footnote, 2 for the second, and so on. Footnote reference numbers are written immediately after the information in the text for which credit is being given. The numbers are small and slightly raised above the line. Most commonly, footnotes are placed at the bottom of the page of the research paper that contains the information or quotation cited, with a horizontal line separating the text from the footnotes.

Examine the sample text and its corresponding footnotes:

> The 1960s were a period of intense political and cultural turmoil in the United States. The war in Vietnam, the peace movement, and the women's liberation movement politicized college campuses.[1] The generation gap was obvious in the music preferences of the younger generation. Joe Rechts, an outspoken conservative political leader, asserted that ". . . rock and roll music is anti-American and encourages our youth to take drugs."[2] Heather Pax, president of the Berkeley Rock Music Fan Club, argued that "Rock music is a form of free speech that allows today's youth to express themselves and develop their own identity."[3]

---

[1]Mary Proff, <u>America's College Students</u> (Newark: Orbis Press, 1966), 17.
[2]Joe Rechts, "The Decline of America's Youth: Censoring Rock and Roll," <u>Doing It Right: The Magazine for Conservative Americans</u>, 18 Jan. 1965.
[3]Heather Pax, "Rock Music as Personal Expression," <u>Rock 'n' Roll Beat</u>, 4 Dec. 1967: 12–14.

Sometimes your teacher will prefer to have all the footnotes on one or more pages at the end of the paper. When footnotes are placed at the end of a paper, the same format is used for writing the footnotes. Ask your teacher where footnotes should be placed in your research paper.

1. Why do you use footnotes in a research paper?

2. In what two places can footnotes be placed?

3. How do you know where footnotes should be placed in your paper?

Read your research paper and add footnotes where necessary.

Preparing the Title Page   7-13

The **title page** is the first page of the research paper. It must include the title of the paper, the date the paper is due, your teacher's name, and the name of the class for which you wrote the paper..

Look at the sample title page. Follow these steps to prepare the title page for your paper. You may use the format provided in this example, or one that your teacher requires.

1. Center and type the title. Use all caps or boldface to highlight it.

2. Three lines below the title, center and type the word *by*. Three lines below the word *by*, center and type your name.

3. Two lines below your name, center and type the date that the paper is due.

4. Four lines from the bottom margin, center and type *For*: followed by your teacher's name and the name of the class for which you wrote the paper.

The History of Rock and Roll

by

Patricia Brown
September 18, 1998

For: Mr. William Hopedale
American History

Preparing the Table of Contents

7-14

The **table of contents** is the second page of the research paper. Look at the sample Table of Contents. Follow these steps to prepare a Table of Contents for your paper.

1. Type "Table of Contents" at the top of a page with the first letter of the word "Table" and the first letter of the word "Contents" capitalized.

2. Type each entry and the page number on which it begins. Capitalize the major words in each entry.

3. Use dashes or periods to connect the entry to its page number.

Table of Contents

	Page
Introduction	1
The Early Years of Rock and Roll	1
Influence of Black Music	2
The R&B Music Scene in Harlem, Memphis, and Chicago	3
The British Influence on Rock and Roll	4
The Beatles, Rolling Stones and Others	4
The Psychedelic Years	5
Drugs and Rock and Roll	6
Rock and Roll and Popular Culture	6
Fashion of Rock Music	8
Women and Rock Music	9
Rock and Roll Around the World	10
Conclusion	11
Bibliography	12

Preparing the Bibliography 7-15

The **bibliography** provides a list of all the sources you used to gather information for your paper. It is placed at the end of your paper.

Look at the sample bibliography. Follow these steps to prepare a bibliography for your paper.

1. Type the word "Bibliography" at the top center of a page.

2. Arrange your bibliography cards in alphabetical order by the first word on each card. (Ignore initial articles such as *A, An*, and *The*.)

3. Type the information as it appears on each bibliography card. Indent the second and following lines as shown on the sample bibliography below.

Bibliography

Aquila, Richard. "A Scholar Takes His Views on Rock 'n' Roll to the Air." *Chronicle of Higher Education* 31 Jan. 1997 : B71+. *UMI Periodical Abstracts*. CD ROM. Ann Arbor, MI: UMI, 1997.

Britain Invades, America Fights Back. Written, produced, and directed by Andrew Solt. Videocassette. Time-Life Video and Television, 1995.

Chappell, Kevin. "How Blacks Invented Rock and Roll: R&B Stars Created Foundations of Multibillion-dollar Industry." *Ebony* Jan.1997: 52–54.

Coppage, Noel. "Rock Music." *Encyclopedia Americana*. 1995 ed.

Friedlander, Paul. *Rock and Roll: A Social History*. Boulder, CO.: Westview Press, 1996.

Pareles, Jon. "Finally Reckoning with Rock History" (Concert at the Opening of the Rock and Roll Hall of Fame in Cleveland, Ohio). *New York Times* 4 Sept. 1995, nat'l ed.: 9.

Poiger, Uta. "Rock 'n' Roll, Female Sexuality, and the Cold War Battle over German Identities." *Journal of Modern History* 68:3 (1996): 577–617.

Rock and Roll Hall of Fame and Museum. *Rockhall.com*. 29 July 1997. Rock and Roll Hall of Fame and Museum. http://www/rockhall.com World Wide Web, Netscape. July 29, 1997.

United States. Congress. Senate. Committee on the Judiciary. Subcommittee on Juvenile Justice. *Shaping Our Responses to Violent and Demeaning Imagery in Popular Music*. Hearing. 103rd Cong., 2nd session. Washington: GPO, 1995.

Final Checklist   7-16

When you have finished writing your research paper, examine it to complete the Final Checklist. Place a ✔ in front of each question for which you can answer YES. If you have a ✔ in front of all questions, your paper is ready to be handed in to your instructor. If not, continue to revise your paper until you have a ✔ in front of all questions. Then your paper is ready to be handed in to your teacher.

Final Checklist

____ Do I have a title page?

____ Do I have a table of contents?

____ Are the pages numbered correctly?

____ Have I included all the footnotes?

____ Does the bibliography include all the sources I used?

____ Do I have a second copy for my files?

Answer Key

7-1 Answers will vary.

7-2 1. Answers will vary, but should show more focused topic, such as "space" narrowed down to a place like "the moon." 2. Responses will vary, but should show a more focused topic, such as immigrants from a specific country, or a particular perspective on immigration, such as legal impressions. 3. Responses will vary, but should show a more focused topic, such as a specific aspect of culture for a specific country in Latin America. 4. Responses will vary.

7-3 1. I. 2. P. 3. P. 4. I. 5. P. 6. P. 7 P. 8. I. 9. P. 10. I. 11. I. 12. I. 13. I. 14. P.

7-4 Answers will vary, but new topics should show a point of view.

7-5 Answers will vary.

7-6 Answers will vary.

7-7 Answers will vary.

7-8 Note cards will vary.

7-9 Outlines will vary.

7-10 Drafts will vary.

7-11 Answers will vary.

7-12 1. When credit must be given to sources from which you take quotations or major ideas. 2. At the bottom of a page or at the end of the paper. 3. Your teacher.

7-13 Title pages will vary.

7-14 Tables of contents will vary.

7-15 Bibliographies will vary.

7-16 Answers will vary.

CHAPTER EIGHT

Using Resources for Oral Presentations

CHAPTER OBJECTIVES

1. Teach students about specialized print and electronic reference sources to use when preparing oral presentations.
2. Teach students to use resources on the WWW to prepare for oral presentations.

TITLES OF REPRODUCIBLE ACTIVITIES

8-1 Locating Print Sources for Quotations
8-2 Using Print Sources for Quotations
8-3 Quotations on the WWW
8-4 Locating Speeches in Print
8-5 Locating Speeches in Audio/Visual Formats
8-6 Locating Sources for Opposing Viewpoints
8-7 Helpful WWW Sources for Oral Presentations
   Answer Key

USING THE REPRODUCIBLE ACTIVITIES

Use activities 8-1 through 8-3 to introduce students to quotation sources in print and on the WWW. Use activities 8-4 and 8-5 to show students how to locate and use sample speeches in print and in audio/visual formats. Activity 8-6 includes sources for opposing viewpoints. Finally, use activity 8-7 to introduce students to information on the WWW related to oral presentations.

8-1 Locating Print Sources for Quotations

Explain to students that they may want to use quotations when preparing oral presentations. For example, they may want to use quotations as a "hook" or to provide humor. Have students read about print sources for quotations. Explain that some quotation sources are general, covering all topics, and others are specialized, for specific topics. Then have students complete 1 through 4 by using the library to find each source listed. Remind students to use the online or card catalog to look up the title of each quotation's source to find its call number and location. Then have students use their library catalog to find a quotation source on a specific topic to complete 5.

8-2 Using Print Sources for Quotations

Have students use a quotation source located in 8-1 to select a quotation on the topics provided. Have students write the quotation, the author of the quotation, the source where they found the quotation, and the page number. Have students share what they learned about using reference sources for quotations.

8-3 Quotations on the WWW

Use this activity only if students have access to the WWW. Students may complete the activity either on their own, or in a lab with your assistance. In 8-2, students used print reference sources for quotations to select quotations on specific topics. Now have students use the WWW to locate and select quotations on the same topics. Have students select one or both of the web sites provided to find quotations on the topics. Tell students to write the quotation, the author of the quotation, the web site where it was found, and the URL for the web site.

8-4 Locating Speeches in Print

Explain to students that they can read speeches to get ideas for "hooking" the audience, making transitions, using humor, and documenting evidence. Tell students about reference sources that contain speeches and other reference sources that are indexes to speeches. Then have students complete the activity by using the library to find each source listed. Remind students to use the online or card catalog to look up each title to find its call number and location.

USING RESOURCES FOR ORAL PRESENTATIONS **177**

8-5 Locating Speeches in Audio/Visual Formats

Explain to students that they can listen to or watch speeches to get ideas for "hooking" the audience, making transitions, using humor, and documenting evidence. Have students go to the library to find a speech in audio/visual format. Then have students complete the activity as they listen to or view the speech they selected. Use the variety of responses to help students understand the various techniques that can be used in oral presentations.

8-6 Locating Sources for Opposing Viewpoints

Explain to students that many oral presentations require the speaker to present a point of view. Have students read about sources for opposing viewpoints. Then have students complete the activity by finding sources for opposing viewpoints located in their library.

You may substitute other sources if your library does not own the titles suggested.

8-7 Helpful WWW Sources for Oral Presentations [C]

Use this activity only if students have access to the WWW. Students may complete the activity either on their own, or in a lab with your assistance. Have students select one of the sites to visit on the WWW. Instruct students to complete the activity by surfing the site and reading, synthesizing, and summarizing important information they find. Remind students to apply what they have learned about navigating a web site.

Locating Print Sources for Quotations 8-1

Print sources for quotations usually have a keyword index. The original source for each quotation is also provided. Some print sources for quotations are general and others are specialized. Print sources for quotations are usually located in the Reference Collection.

General print sources for quotations include quotations on a wide variety of topics. Here are some common print sources for quotations.

> *Oxford Dictionary of Quotations*
> *Familiar Quotations: A Collection of Passages, Phrases and Proverbs Traced to Their Sources in Ancient and Modern Times (Bartlett's)*
> *Magill's Quotations in Context*
> *Harper Book of American Quotations*

Look up these titles in your library. Write the title and call number of those sources owned by your library. If provided, write the location after the call number.

1. Title:

   Call number:

2. Title:

   Call number:

3. Title:

   Call number:

4. Title:

   Call number:

Specialized print sources for quotations include quotations for specific subjects, for example *Political Quotations*. Use your library catalog to identify a specialized quotations source for a topic of your choice and complete the following.

5. Title:

   Call number:

Using Print Sources for Quotations

Use a quotation source to select a quotation on each of the following topics. You may need to look in more than one source to find your topic. For each topic, write the quotation selected and the name of the author you are quoting. Also include the title of the quotation's source and the page number(s) where the quotation appears in the source.

1. **Topic: marriage**

    Quotation:

    Author of quote:

    Title of quotation source:

    Page number:

2. **Topic: books**

    Quotation:

    Author of quote:

    Title of quotation source:

    Page number:

3. **Topic: government**

    Quotation:

    Author of quote:

    Title of quotation source:

    Page number:

Quotations on the WWW   8-3

Quotation sources can be found in electronic as well as in print formats. There are several major sites for quotations on the WWW. Two frequently used web sites for quotations are:

Project Bartleby: http://www.cc.columbia.edu/acis/bartleby/bartlett/
The Quotations Page: http://www.starlingtech.com/quotes/

Visit one or more of these web sites to find quotations on the following topics. For each topic, write the quotation selected and the person you are quoting. Also include the title of the web site and its URL.

1. **Topic: marriage**

   Quotation:

   Author of quote:

   Title of web site:

   URL:

2. **Topic: books**

   Quotation:

   Author of quote:

   Title of web site:

   URL:

3. **Topic: government**

   Quotation:

   Author of quote:

   Title of web site:

   URL:

4. Describe your experience using quotation sources on the WWW compared to those in print.

Locating Speeches in Print   8-4

Reading speeches can help you prepare for oral presentations. You can read speeches to get ideas for:

- Opening lines and/or "hooks"
- Transitions
- Using humor
- Including research data

There are several important print sources that contain speeches. Some of the most frequently used sources of speeches are:

Representative American Speeches
A Treasury of Great American Speeches
Vital Speeches of the Day

Look up these titles in your library. Write down each title and call number if owned. Include a location with the call number if provided.

1. Title:

    Call number:

2. Title:

    Call number:

3. Title:

    Call number:

Some reference sources are indexes to speeches. They list citations for sources where the speech can be found. Here are two such indexes:

- *Speech Index*: An index to collections of world-famous orations and speeches for various occasions
- *We Shall Be Heard*: An index to speeches by American women

Look up these titles in your library. Write down each title and call number if owned. Include a location with the call number if provided.

4. Title:

    Call number:

5. Title:

    Call number:

Copyright © 1999 by Allyn and Bacon.

181

Locating Speeches in Audio/Visual Formats

8-5

Many libraries have audio and/or video cassettes of famous speeches. Reviewing such speeches can often help you prepare for your oral presentations.

Use your library catalog and/or the audio/visual section of your library to obtain an audio or video cassette of a speech. Review the speech and answer the questions.

1. Did you use an audio or video cassette?

2. Who is the speaker?

3. What is the topic of the speech?

4. Describe the hook the speaker used to engage the audience.

5. Describe how humor was used.

6. Describe how quotations were used.

7. Describe the type of research data used.

8. Describe something you thought was effective about the speaker's voice.

9. If you viewed a video, describe something you thought was effective about the speaker's use of body language.

Locating Sources for Opposing Viewpoints

8-6

Sources for opposing viewpoints identify current controversial topics and include various points of view. Sources for opposing viewpoints will help you prepare for persuasive oral presentations and debates.

1. A frequently used source for opposing viewpoints is *CQ Researcher*. *CQ Researcher* provides pros and cons for controversial topics. Look up *CQ Researcher* in your library. Write the title and call number. If provided, include a location after the call number.

    Title:

    Call number:

2. Editorials in newspapers are another important source for viewpoints on controversial topics. An important source for editorials on specific topics is *Editorials on File*. Each issue of *Editorials on File* is a collection of editorials on a specific topic. Locate two issues of *Editorials on File* in your library catalog. For each issue, write the topic.

    Topic:

    Topic:

3. Another frequently used source is the *Opposing Viewpoints* series of books. Each book is on a specific controversial topic and has its own title. Look up *Opposing Viewpoints* in your library catalog and write the names of two titles.

    Title:

    Title:

Helpful WWW Sources for Oral Presentations

8-7

Here is a list of web sites with information that might be useful when preparing oral presentations.

Speaker's Companion Reference Page
http://www.lm.com/~chipp/spkrref.htm

Allyn and Bacon Public Speaking web site
http://www.abacon.com/pubspeak/index.htm

A.U.D.I.E.N.C.E Analysis
http://www.ljlseminars.com/audience.htm

Speech Anxiety
http://www.rmit.usf.edu/counsel/self-hlp/speech.htm

Fear of Public Speaking
http://www.access.digex.net/~nuance/fearspk1.html

American Communication Association
http://www.americancomm.org

Select one of these web sites to explore. Type in the URL and use your navigating skills to explore the site. Write a statement that tells what you learned about making oral presentations.

Answer Key

8-1 Answers will vary.
8-2 Answers will vary.
8-3 Answers will vary.
8-4 Answers will vary.
8-5 Answers will vary.
8-6 Answers will vary.
8-7 Answers will vary.

Bibliography

Teaching Information Literacy

Barclay, D. A. *Teaching Electronic Information Literacy: A How-to-Do-It Manual*. New York: Neal-Schuman, 1995.

Barnett, D. *Research It! Write It! A Step by Step Guide to Research and Writing* (2nd ed.). Fort Atkinson, WI: Alleyside Press, 1997.

Bleakley, A., & Carrigan, J. *Resource-Based Learning Activities: Information Literacy for High School Students*. Chicago: American Library Association, 1994.

Conan, M., & Heavers, K. *What You Need to Know about Developing Study Skills, Taking Notes and Tests, Using Dictionaries and Libraries*. Lincolnwood, IL: National Textbook Company, 1994.

Druce, A. *Library Lessons for Grades 7–9*. Lanham, MD: Scarecrow Press, 1997.

Garrett, L. J., & Moore, J. *Teaching Library Skills in the Middle and High School: A How-to-Do-It Manual*. New York: Neal-Schuman, 1993.

Iannuzzi, P., Mangrum, C. T. II, & Strichart, S. S. *Teaching Study Skills and Strategies in College*. Boston: Allyn and Bacon, 1998.

Joyce, M. Z., & Tallman, J. I. *Making the Writing and Research Connection with the I-search Process: A How-to-Do-It Manual for Teachers and School Librarians*. New York: Neal-Schuman, 1996.

Kuhlthau, C. C. *Teaching the Library Research Process* (2nd ed.). Metuchen, NJ: Scarecrow Press, 1994.

List, Carla. *Introduction to Library Research* (2nd ed.). New York: McGraw-Hill, 1993.

McCarthy, M. J. *Mastering the Information Age: A Course in Working Smarter, Thinking Better, and Learning Faster*. New York: Tacher, 1990.

McInerney, C. F. *Find It!: The Inside Story at Your Library*. Minneapolis, MN: Lerner Publications, 1989.

Meister, T. *Pardon Me, but Your References Are Showing!* (2nd ed.). Fort Atkinson, WI: Alleyside Press, 1996.

Mendrinos, R. *Building Information Literacy Using High Technology: A Guide for Schools and Libraries*. Englewood, CO: Libraries Unlimited, 1994.

Moody, R. B. *Coming to Terms: Subject Search Strategies in the School Library Media Center*. New York: Neal-Schuman, 1995.

Roach, C., & Moore, J. *Teaching Library Skills in Grades K through 6: A How-to-Do-It Manual*. New York: Neal-Schuman, 1993.

Strichart, S. S., Mangrum, C. T. II, & Iannuzzi, P. *Teaching Study Skills and Strategies to High School Students*. Boston: Allyn and Bacon, 1997.

Wolf, C. E. *Basic Library Skills* (2nd ed.). Jefferson, NC: McFarland, 1986.

About Information Literacy

American Library Association. American Association of School Libraries. AASL/AECT National Guidelines Vision Committee. *Information Literacy Standards for Student Learning*. October 7, 1996. http://www.ala.org/aasl/stndsdrft5.html World Wide Web, Netscape. January 16, 1998.

American Library Association. American Association of School Libraries. *Position Paper on Information Literacy*. Copyright 1993, Wisconsin Educational Media Association. http://www.ala.org/aasl/positions/PS_infolit.html World Wide Web, Netscape. January 16, 1998.

American Library Association. Presidential Committee on Information Literacy. *Final Report*. 17 April 1995. gopher://ala1.ala.org:70/00/alagophiv/50417007.document World Wide Web, Netscape. January 16, 1998.

Amstutz, D., & Whitson, D. "University Faculty and Information Literacy: Who Teaches the Students?" *Research Strategies*, 15(1) (Winter 1997): 18–25

Atton, C. F. "Using Critical Thinking as a Basis for Library User Education." *The Journal of Academic Librarianship*, 20(5–6) (November 1994): 310–313.

Barron, D. D. "If All Roads Lead to Rome, Why Are We in Athens?: School Library Media Programs and National Standards." *School Library Media Activities Monthly*, 14(1) (September 1997): 47–50.

Bjorner, S. N. "The Information Literacy Curriculum: A Working Model." *IATUL Quarterly*, 5(1) (1991): 150–160.

Blandy, S. G. "The Librarian's Role in Academic Assessment and Accreditation: A Case Study." *The Reference Librarian*, 38 (1992): 69–87.

Branch, K. A. "Library Instruction and Information Literacy in Community and Technical Colleges." *RQ*, 35(4) (Summer 1996): 476–483.

Breivik, P. S. "Information Literacy: Educating Children for the 21st Century." *Scholastic* (1994): 198.

Breivik, P. S. "Information Literacy: When Computers Aren't Enough." *Learning and Leading with Technology*, 23 (February 1996): 65–67.

Bruce, C. S. "Information Literacy: A Framework for Higher Education." *Australian Library Journal*, 44(3) (August 1995):158–170.

California Association of Academic and Research Libraries. CARL Task Force to Recommend Information Literacy Standard to WASC. *Draft recommendations to WASC on an Information Literacy Standard.* 29 Sept 1997. http://www.carl-acrl.org/Reports/rectoWASC.html World Wide Web, Netscape. January 16, 1998.

California School Library Association. *From Library Skills to Information Literacy: A Handbook for the 21st Century.* Castle Rock, CO: Hi Willow Research and Publishing, 1997.

Colorado Department of Education. *Colorado Information Literacy Guidelines.* http://cde.state.co.us/infolitg.htm September 1994. World Wide Web, Netscape. January 16, 1998.

Crane, B. "A Model for Teaching Critical Thinking through Online Searching." *The Reference Librarian, 44* (1994): 41–52.

Daragan, P. "Developing Lifelong Learners: An Integrative and Developmental Approach to Information Literacy." *Research Strategies, 14*(2) (Spring 1996): 68–81.

Doyle, C. "Information Literacy in an Information Society. A Concept for the Information Age." ERIC 1994.

Eisenberg, M. B., & Johnson, D. "Computer Skills for Information Problem-Solving: Learning and Teaching Technology in Context." Washington, DC: ERIC Clearinghouse, ERIC Document 392463, March 1996.

Farmer, L. "Workshops for Teachers: Becoming Partners for Information Literacy." Worthington, OH: Linworth, 1995.

Farmer, L. S. J. "Authentic Assessment of Information Literacy through Electronic Products." *Book Report, 16* (September–October 1997): 11–13.

Fernandez, G. "Critical Thinking in Library User Education." *Florida Libraries, 38* (October 1995): 124.

Ford, B. J., & Breivik, P. S. "Learning through Information Literacy." *American Libraries, 24*(1) (January 1993): 987.

Frappaolo, C. "Planning for the Information Revolution." *Information Today, 10*(4) (April 1993): 17–18.

George, M. W. "Information Literacy: A Selective Review of Recent Literature." *New Jersey Libraries, 26*(1) (1993): 3–4.

George, M. W., Kuhlthau, C., & Nash, S. "Information Literacy and Critical Thinking: Definitions and Distinctions." *New Jersey Libraries, 26*(1) (1993): 2–26.

George, R., & Luke, R. "The Critical Place of Information Literacy in the Trend towards Flexible Delivery in Higher Education Contexts." *Australian Academic and Research Libraries, 27*(3) (September 1996): 204–212.

Gibson, G. "Critical Thinking: Implications for Instruction." *RQ, 35*(1) (Fall 1995): 27–35.

Grassian, E. *National Information Literacy Initiative: Student Information Literacy Competencies.* American Library Association, Association of College and Research Libraries, National Information Literacy Initiative. 10 November 1997. http://www.ala.org/acrl/nili/ilcompt.html World Wide Web, Netscape. January 16, 1998.

Greer, A., Weston, L., & Alm, M. "Assessment of Learning Outcomes: A Measure of Progress in Library Literacy." *College and Research Libraries, 52*(6) (November 1991): 549–557.

Hancock, V. E. "Information Literacy, Brain-Based Learning, and the Technological Revolution: Implications for Education." *School Library Media Activities Monthly, 12*(1) (September 1995): 31–34.

Iannuzzi, P. "Assessing Libraries in Support of Campus Missions: The Information Literacy Imperative." Paper presented at the American Association of Higher Education Annual Conference on Assessment and Quality, Miami Beach, FL. 1997. http://www.fiu.edu/~library/ili/iliaahe.html World Wide Web, Netscape. April 5, 1998.

Johnson, D. A., & Eisenberg, M. B. "Computer Literacy and Information Literacy: A Natural Combination." *Emergency Librarian, 23*(5) (May–June 1996): 12–16.

Kautzman, A. M. "Teaching Critical Thinking: The Alliance of Composition Studies and Research Instruction." *Reference Services Review, 24*(3) (1996): 61–66.

Kunkel, L. R., Waver, S. M., & Cook, K. N. "What Do They Know? An Assessment of Undergraduate Library Skills." *Journal of Academic Librarianship, 22*(6) (November 1996): 430–434.

LaGuardia, C., et al. *Teaching the New Library: A How-to-Do-It Manual for Planning and Designing Instructional Programs.* New York: Neal-Schuman, 1996.

Lawton, B. "Library Instruction Needs Assessment: Designing Survey Instruments." *Research Strategies, 7*(3) (Summer 1989): 119–128.

Martorana, J., & Doyle, C. "Computers on, Critical Thinking Off: Challenges of Teaching in the Electronic Environment." *Research Strategies, 14*(3) (Summer 1996): 184–191.

McCrank, L. J. "Information Literacy: A Bogus Bandwagon?" *Library Journal, 116*(8) (May 1991): 38.

Mensching, T. E. *Coping with Information Illiteracy: Bibliographic Instruction for the Information Age.* Ann Arbor, MI: Pierian Press, 1990.

Morrison, H. "Information Literacy Skills: An Exploratory Focus Group Study of Student Perceptions." *Research Strategies, 15*(1) (Winter 1997): 4–17.

Mullins, L. S. "Partnerships in Information Teaching and Learning: Building a Collaborative Culture in the University Community." *New Jersey Libraries, 26* (1993): 18.

Neal, J. G. "Academic Libraries: 2000 and Beyond." *Library Journal, 121*(12) (July 1996): 74–76.

Oregon Educational Media Association. *Oregon Information Literacy Guidelines.* http://www.teleport.com/~oema/infolit.html February 1997. World Wide Web, Netscape. January 16, 1998.

Rader, H. B. "Information Literacy and the Undergraduate Curriculum." *Library Trends, 44*(2) (Fall 1995): 270–278.

Ratteray, O. M. T., & Simmons, H. L. "Information Literacy in Higher Education: A Report on the Middle States Region." Washington, DC: ERIC Clearinghouse, ERIC Document 388136, September 1995.

Read This First: An Owner's Guide to the New Model Statement of Objectives for Academic Bibliographic Instruction. Chicago: American Library Association, 1991.

Rettig, J. "The Convergence of the Twain or Titanic Collision? BI and Reference in the 1990s Sea of Change." *Reference Service Review, 23*(1) (Spring 1995): 7–20.

Ross, T. W., & Bailey, G. D. "Wanted: A New Literacy for the Information Age." *NASSP Bulletin, 78*(563) (September 1994): 31–35.

Schultz, C. L. "Development of an Information Literacy Course for Community College Students." Dissertation, Virginia Polytechnic Institute and State University, 1995.

Shapiro, J. J., & Hughes, S. K. "Information Literacy as a Liberal Art." *EDUCOM Review, 31*(2) (March/April, 1996) http://www.educom.edu/web/pubs/review/reviewArticles/31231.html World Wide Web, Netscape. January 16, 1998.

Smith, J. B. *Achieving a Curriculum Based Library Media Center Program.* Chicago: American Library Association, 1995.

Snavely, L., & Cooper, N. "The Information Literacy Debate." *Journal of Academic Librarianship, 23*(1) (January 1997): 9–14.

Strege, K. "Information Literacy." *PNLA Quarterly, 61* (Winter 1997): 18–20.

Tierney, J. "Information Literacy and a College Library: A Continuing Experiment." *New Directions for Higher Education, 20*(2) (Summer 1992): 63–71.

Turrell, L. "Library Online! A Guide to Computer Research." Washington, DC: ERIC Clearinghouse, ERIC Document 400830, 1997.

Walster, D., & Welborn, L. "Colorado's Information Literacy Guidelines." *School Library Media Activities Monthly, 12* (March 1996): 23–27.

Walster, D. Student-Centered Information Literacy Programs: The Colorado Vision. *School Library Media Annual (SLMA), 13* (1995): 45–53.

Warmkessel, M. M., & McCade, J. M. "Integrating Information Literacy into the Curriculum." *Research Strategies, 15*(2) (1997): 80–88.

Wolf, C., & Wolf, R. *Basic Library Skills* (3rd ed.). Jefferson, NC: McFarland & Co., 1993.

Zenor, S. D. "AECT/AASL National Guidelines: The Update of Information Power." *Tech Trends, 42*(1) (January–February 1997): 2.

APPENDIX A

Information Literacy Curriculum

INTRODUCTION

The ability to access and use information is necessary for success in school, work and personal life. The following steps represent the basic element in an information literacy curriculum.

I. DEFINING THE NEED FOR INFORMATION

The first step in the information problem solving process is to recognize that an information need exists and to define that need. The student will be able to:

   A. Recognize different uses of information (i.e. occupational, intellectual, recreational)
   B. Place the information needed within a frame of reference (who, what, when, where, how, why)
   C. Relate the information needed to prior knowledge
   D. Formulate the information problem using a variety of questioning skills (i.e. yes/no, open ended)

II. INITIATING THE SEARCH STRATEGY

Once the information problem has been formulated, the student must understand that a plan for searching has to be developed. The student will be able to:

   A. Determine what information is needed, often through a series of sub-questions

---

Source: Developed by the Wisconsin Education Media Association (WEMA) and adopted by the American Association of School Librarians, a division of ALA. Reprinted with permission from WEMA.

B. Brainstorm ideas and recognize a variety of visual ways of organize ideas to visualize relationships among them (i.e. webbing, outlining, listing)
C. Select and use a visual organizer appropriate to subject
D. List key words, concepts, subject headings, descriptors
E. Explain the importance of using more than one source of information
F. Identify potential sources of information
G. Identify the criteria for evaluating possible sources (i.e. timeliness, format, appropriateness)

III. LOCATING THE RESOURCES

At the onset of a search a student will recognize the importance of locating information from a variety of sources and accessing specific information found within an individual resource. The student will be able to:

A. Locate print, audiovisual, and computerized resources in the school library media center using catalogs and other bibliographic tools
B. Locate information outside of the school library media center through online databases, interlibrary loan, telephone and facsimile technology
C. Identify and use community information agencies (i.e. public and academic libraries, government offices) to locate additional resources
D. Use people as sources of information through interviews, surveys and letters of inquiry
E. Consult with library media specialists and teachers to assist in identifying sources of information
F. Access specific information within resources by using internal organizers (i.e. indexes, tables of contents, cross references) and electronic search strategies (i.e. keywords, Boolean logic)

IV. ASSESSING AND COMPREHENDING THE INFORMATION

Once potentially useful information has been located, the student uses a screening process to determine the usefulness of the information. The student will be able to:

A. Skim and scan for major ideas and keywords to identify relevant information
B. Differentiate between primary and secondary sources
C. Determine the authoritativeness, currentness and reliability of the information

D. Differentiate among fact, opinion, propaganda, point of view, and bias
E. Recognize errors in logic
F. Recognize omissions, if any, in information
G. Classify, group or label the information
H. Recognize interrelationships among concepts
I. Differentiate between cause and effect
J. Identify points of agreement and disagreement among sources
K. Select information in formats most appropriate to the student's individual learning style
L. Revise and redefine the information problem if necessary

V. INTERPRETING THE INFORMATION

Following an assessment of the information, the student must use the information to solve the particular information problem. The student will be able to:

A. Summarize the information in the student's own words; paraphrase or quote important facts and details when necessary for accuracy and clarity
B. Synthesize newly gathered information with previous information
C. Organize and analyze information in a new way
D. Compare information gathered with the original problem and adjust strategies, locate additional information or re-examine information when necessary
E. Draw conclusions based on the information gathered and the student's interpretation of it

VI. COMMUNICATING THE INFORMATION

The student must be able to organize and communicate the results of the information problem-solving effort. The student will be able to:

A. Use the search information to identify the important conclusions or resolutions to the problem to be shared with others
B. Decide on a purpose (i.e. to inform, persuade, entertain) for communicating the information and identify
C. Choose a format (i.e. written, oral, visual) appropriate for the audience and purpose
D. Create an original product (i.e. speech, research paper, videotape, drama)
E. Provide appropriate documentation (i.e. bibliography) and comply with copyright law

VII. EVALUATING THE PRODUCT AND PROCESS

Evaluation is the ability to determine how well the final product resolved the information problem and if the steps taken to reach the desired outcome were appropriate and efficient. Students may evaluate their own work and/or be evaluated by others (i.e. classmates, teachers, library media staff, parents). The student will be able to:

A. Determine the extent to which the conclusions and project met the defined information need and/or satisfied the assignment (i.e. how well did I do?)

B. Consider if the research question/problem, search strategy, resources, or interpretation should have been expanded, revised or otherwise modified (i.e. what could/should I have done differently?)

C. Re-assess his/her understanding of the process and identify steps which need further understanding, skill development, or practice (i.e. how can I do better in the future?)

Notes

Notes

Order Form

Information Literacy Assessment (ILA)

MANGRUM-STRICHART LEARNING RESOURCES

Schools/Libraries:
Individuals:
Librarians/Media Specialists:

Ordering Information:
Enclose purchase order number, authorized signature and title.
Orders must be prepaid. Please enclose check or money order.
You may order as an individual or your Library will be billed if you provide an approved purchase order number.

Quantity	Item	Price	Subtotal
_____	ILA disk with unlimited administrations License for installation on 1 computer	$ 99.95	_____
_____	ILA disk with unlimited administrations License for installation on 2-5 computers	$ 199.95	_____
_____	ILA disk with unlimited administrations License for installation on 6-30 computers	$ 499.95	_____

Florida Residents add 6% Sales Tax..
_____ or include Tax Exempt Number_____
Shipping and Handling.........$4.95 for first disk; $1.95 for each additional disk

Check format desired: Windows____ Macintosh____   **TOTAL** [____]

Method of Payment -- check one
☐ Check enclosed for _____
☐ Money order enclosed for_____
☐ Bill us. Purchase order No._____
(Schools Only -- Purchase order with authorized signature and title enclosed)

Send all orders to:

MANGRUM-STRICHART LEARNING
RESOURCES
Order Department   Fax: 305-252-4699
9841 SW 122 Street   Voice Mail: 305-233-6791
Miami, FL 33176

Please make check or money order payable to:

MANGRUM-STRICHART LEARNING
RESOURCES
prices subject to change

Thank you for your order!

A companion book containing reproducible activities, **Teaching Information Literacy Skills**, is available from: Allyn and Bacon Order Department, P.O. Box 10695, Des Moines, IA 56336-0695 or call 1-800-278-3525.

Ship to: *(Please print)*
Name_____
School_____
Address_____
City_____
State_____Zip_____
Telephone No. (_____)_____

Bill to: *(Please print)*
Name_____
School_____
Address_____
City_____
State_____Zip_____
Purchase Order No._____
Telephone No. (_____)_____

LICENSING AGREEMENT

You should carefully read the following terms and conditions before opening this disk package. Opening this disk package indicates your acceptance of these terms and conditions. If you do not agree with them, you should promptly return the package unopened.

Allyn and Bacon provides this Program and License its use. You assume responsibility for the selection of the Program to achieve your intended results, and for the installation, use, and results obtained from the Program. This License extends only to use of the Program in the United States or countries in which the Program is marketed by duly authorized distributors.

License Grant

You hereby accept a nonexclusive, nontransferable, permanent License to install and use the Program on a single computer at any given time. You may copy the Program solely for backup or archival purposes in support of your use of the Program on the single computer. You may not modify, translate, disassemble, decompile, or reverse engineer the Program, in whole or in part.

Term

This License is effective until terminated. Allyn and Bacon reserves the right to terminate this License automatically if any provision of the License is violated. You may terminate the License at any time. To terminate this License, you must return the Program, including documentation, along with a written warranty stating that all copies of the Program in your possession have been returned or destroyed.

Limited Warranty

The Program is provided "As Is" without warranty of any kind, either express or implied, including, but not limited to, the implied warranties or merchantability and fitness for a particular purpose. The entire risk as to the quality and performance of the Program is with you. Should the Program prove defective, you (and not Allyn and Bacon or any authorized distributor) assume the entire cost of all necessary servicing, repair, or correction. No oral or written information or advice given by Allyn and Bacon, its dealers, distributors, or agents shall create a warranty or increase the scope of its warranty.

Some states do not allow the exclusion of implied warranty, so the above exclusion may not apply to you. This warranty gives you specific legal rights and you may also have other rights that vary from state to state.

Allyn and Bacon does not warrant that the functions contained in the Program will meet your requirements or that the operation of the Program will be uninterrupted or error free.

However, Allyn and Bacon warrants the disk(s) on which the Program is furnished to be free from defects in material and workmanship under normal use for a period of ninety (90) days form the date of delivery to you as evidenced by a copy of your receipt.

The Program should not be relied on as the sole basis to solve a problem whose incorrect solution could result in injury to a person or property. If the Program is employed in such a manner, it is at the user's own risk and Allyn and Bacon explicitly disclaims all liability for such misuse.

Limitation of Remedies

Allyn and Bacon's entire liability and your exclusive remedy shall be:

1. The replacement of any disk not meeting Allyn and Bacon's "Limited Warranty" and that is returned to Allyn and Bacon or

2. If Allyn and Bacon is unable to deliver a replacement disk or cassette that is free of defects in materials or workmanship, you may terminate this Agreement by returning the Program.

In no event will Allyn and Bacon be liable to you for any damages, including any lost profits, lost savings, or other incidental or consequential damages arising out of the use or inability to use such Program even if Allyn and Bacon or an authorized distributor has been advised of the possibility of such damages of for any claim by any other party.

Some states do not allow the limitation or exclusion of liability for incidental or consequential damages, so the above limitation or exclusion may not apply to you.

General

You may not sublicense, assign, or transfer the License of the Program. Any attempt to sublicense, assign, or transfer any of the rights, duties, or obligations hereunder is void.

This Agreement will be governed by the laws of the State of Massachusetts.

Should you have any questions concerning this Agreement, or any questions concerning technical support, you may contact Allyn and Bacon by writing to:

Allyn and Bacon
Simon and Schuster Education Group
160 Gould Street
Needham Heights, MA 02194

You acknowledge that you have read this Agreement, understand it, and agree to be bound by its terms and conditions. You further agree that it is the complete and exclusive statement of the Agreement between us that supersedes any proposal or prior Agreement, oral or written, and any other communications between us relating to the subject matter of this Agreement.

Notice to Government End Users

The Program is provided with restricted rights. Use, duplication, or disclosure by the Government is subject to restrictions set forth in subdivison (b)(3)(iii) of The Rights in Technical Data and Computer Software Clause 252.227-7013.